The Hidden Truths

of a

MODERN SEER

First published by Asherah Books, 2015

A CIP catalogue record for this book is available from the British Library.

ISBN-13: 978-1909187863

The Hidden Truths

of a

MODERN SEER

Cher Chevalier

Asherah Books
London

CONTENTS

PREFACE

In this second book of the *Modern Seer Trilogy*, I reveal the grave – yet beautiful and giant – steps that I have taken on the Path to Spiritual Mastery. These further revelations of my journey may seem to some too fantastical to be real. Indeed, they would to me had I not lived them myself!

Seven years have passed since I wrote the manuscript for my first book, *The Hidden Secrets of a Modern Seer*. As I lay bare my *Hidden Truths* in this book, it is my wish that the information disclosed herein may only reach true spiritual aspirants, and only used to assist in the creation of a Divine humanity.

I also wish to express that, although my work as a Spiritual Adviser helping clients from all walks of life continues, my time is now primarily given to writing and to teaching my students around the world who are on the Spiritual Path. I hope you will enjoy this very honest book.

Love and blessings, Cher x
<u>www.spiritualadviser.co.uk</u>

INTRODUCTION

It is written that it takes three and a half years to break the lower self, and a further three and a half years to fully transcend the darkness within so as to be considered fit to embark upon the Path of Spiritual Mastery.

The Hidden Secrets of a Modern Seer, the first book of this trilogy, was completed at the end of my initial three and a half year training period. I'd assumed my whole life from the age of four, when I had my first near-death experience, to have been a spiritual training period, but apparently it was not. In esoteric training, the period is considered to begin when one meets one's earthly Spiritual Teacher: in my case, my African Teacher, Ray.

I survived the first three and a half years training. Some do not. It is true that many students do not make it – quitting for many and varied reasons – and it is also true that some students die during the training. There were many times when I believed I would die, or at least go mad, as some others on the path do. But, by the grace of God, and with the powerful assistance of The Great One, and Ray, I continued on and completed my seven years of training.

The seven years of intense purification, tests and trials is for the purpose of transmuting one's own karma, and ultimately leads one to become karma-free, living harmlessly, on the Path of Self Mastery.

It is on this Path of Self Mastery that one lives in tune with Divine Will, and can – if and when sanctioned and necessary – display powers and perform what others would consider to be miracles. One comes to learn the difference between karma, destiny, and free will, and, having transmuted the shadow nature of the lower self, can become its master and thus master of oneself.

In the Mystery Schools for Initiates on the Path of Self Mastery, much is taught by Beings and Intelligences in the hidden realms. Everything that one thinks, says and does either builds light or builds darkness – quite a responsibility to live with!

As a spy in this world and a team member of a higher order for The Divine Plan, one learns to respond to Divine command and instruction as one lives multidimensionally, as an Initiate, until one becomes a Master!

Mystics, Masters and Great Spiritual Teachers all over the world, irrespective of religious affiliation, race and culture, are in regular telepathic attunement with each other. Having grounded their being in the all- encompassing transcendent spiritual principle, they are able to use their insights as a guide to action in the public domain in whatever station of life they may be. By so doing they assist other sentient beings (not just humans), both in the visible and invisible realms of creation, to evolve and achieve illumination in tune with Divine Purpose. This is the work of The Great Guardians of Evolution.

For the purpose of lighting the way for fellow pilgrims and spiritual aspirants on the path, I will begin where I left off in my first *Modern Seer* book.

CHAPTER 1
ADVANCED TRAINING

My Teacher Ray had said to me, "The Holy Ones have promoted you, Cher," when he likened what I had been enduring for the first three and a half year period to SAS-style training. But he had added, "If you wish to become a disciple of The Path, Cher, it means a lot of work. You have been warned." I had come through the rough terrain but I was not yet an Initiate ready for the Path of Spiritual Mastery.

It was now time for the Being that I previously named in the first *Modern Seer* book as 'The Great One', who now I will reveal, and henceforth refer to, as Em, to fully take the lead. Em had made it clear to me that I was now 'with him' to continue on my training and that we would be 'working from the inside.' Ray would still be in my life but, as had been predicted years ago, he would take more of a back seat. I was also instructed to streamline my energies on to purely spiritual matters.

Psychic experiences and prophecies and predictions are very important, yet are only the tip; the first stages on the path leading to Spiritual Illumination. Psychic and mediumistic experiences are a necessary stage, but beyond them is the Ultimate. Near-death experiences, psychic flashes and spirit communications act as 'triggers' for those who are destined to or choose to walk the spiritual path. But the Path of Mastery, that is lit by The Great Guardians of Evolution, requires pure spiritual alignment.

My daily life of working to assist clients, writing and occasionally appearing in the media, continued as before. But my inner life was to deepen dramatically. The ineffable bliss of being in The Divine Presence increased as the days passed. The states of multidimensionality – awareness of, and functioning in, this and the invisible realm simultaneously – became a regular occurrence. Telepathic communication between myself and other mystics, both in this world and in other worlds, was so frequent it was becoming normal.

Many of the tests during the first three and a half years of my training had involved harrowing psychic attacks and frequent paranormal experiences. In the coming years, the tests were to be more emotional and psychological. Battles of will, if you will. I had to learn to transmute not just the shadow that was left in me, but also my own personal will. I had been told to focus on having a family life, which I was determined to do if it were the will of the Divine. I had remained celibate since breaking my celibacy vow a few years back, and although I was more at peace than I'd ever believed I could be, the loneliness and isolation of my training was still, at times, overwhelmingly frustrating.

As I sat with Ray over dinner one evening (I still met up with him periodically in London), I expressed my frustration at being alone if I was 'supposed' to have a family. Ray sighed and gave me one of his looks as he rolled his eyes and said, "Experiment if you must." But he did not seem pleased. He added that the gifts flowing through me could not be fully utilised until later in life, when I had established my family life, after which deeper spiritual work would take place. Em kept saying that I should remember to lead a family life, yet wasn't keen to help with my endeavours to do so. I had no idea why at the time, but it would all become clear soon enough.

A short while later, I briefly went on dates with a vegetarian man who was an animal lover. Having these two important things in common, I was hopeful there was a chance we could get along. But as I spent time with him, some of his

5

dark secrets were being revealed to me psychically. I had not been focusing too much on the psychic side of my gifts as I'd been instructed to streamline my energies onto spiritual alignment. But the information kept creeping through. Suffice it to say, the friendship was cut off, and for good reason.

Em was not at all sympathetic regarding my emotional needs, and Ray had hinted rather curtly that I may be back again at the 'waters of contradiction.' I was confused, so I decided to shift my attention to the all-important task of pure spiritual alignment. After all, if it was God's will for me to have a family life, it would manifest, with or without my help, right? Wrong. I still had much to learn...

As mentioned at the close of my first *Modern Seer* book, I was now admitted, as a junior, into places of training and worship in the higher – or heavenly – realm. At first, I was always accompanied by Em. I should explain here also that, unbelievable as it sounds, much of my training with Em now involved me being 'in' him or him being 'in' me – as a part of each other's light is the best way that I can describe it. I am struggling with vocabulary here! Em would literally sit within my being and, at times, invite me to sit within his being.

Em would also perform various rituals, including breathing on me or in me. He also gave me tasks and tests to complete, one of which was for me to use the Holy Ash I had been given, in seven specific places: I made a slight mistake in where I put the Ash on one occasion and had terrible nightmares until I placed it in exactly the places Em had instructed me to. This was a very minor thing, but he kept saying that the training now was all in the details.

Em was supportive, but very strict. He continuously stated the importance of holiness and trustworthiness. And added that, just as Ray had said in the past, I would soon need to move up spiritually so I would be able to lift and transmute a part of someone's karma, if that was deserved and sanctioned. It was not enough that I should only be able transmute my own shadow: the work of The Great Ones is to lift and bring other Beings up with them. And they do not compromise the spiritual laws for anyone. Darkness must become light. And light must be used to transmute the darkness.

Em also expressed the need for an aspirant to be cheerful; happiness and joy being a vital part of being spiritual. He went on to say, "You have great authority, and safe passage. Be cheerful!" Then quickly added, "You are only to use the powers that come through you for God's will. You are being prepared to be used by The Divine."

Em and I being merged in one another as light during training sessions soon became usual, but I had noticed that the pains in my body were increasing. Em is a powerful Being and his energy during these initial inner training sessions made my spirit very strong, but my body weak.

In just one of my many experiences of being with – or more accurately, in – Em in the higher realm, we were in a marble-floored room, filled with light, where many beings (human, non-human, and angelic) were worshipping God. Em spoke in me quietly, saying, "We are with The Divine's Shining Ones."

All aspirants of esoteric training know that secrets must be kept secret unless and until one is instructed to reveal them – which may never happen. And herein lies the test. It is no longer so much that one is learning to build one's faith and trust in God and The Divine's helpers. It is more that God and the Divine helpers need to know that you can be trusted. And on that note I was encouraged to go out socialising with friends, to a nightclub of all places, something I hadn't done in quite some time.

I have learned that there is always a higher motive behind

everything I am guided to do, and the nightclub experience was no exception. I had been in the music-filled atmosphere, dancing and enjoying myself for a while when the real reason behind my being there (unbeknown to me beforehand) came flooding into my awareness. A man had caught my attention as I left the dance floor and went to rejoin my friends. He reached out his hand to make my acquaintance and as I heard him say, "hello," the words spilled out of my mouth that the rest of his life belonged to God: he had wasted his life up to this point on evil doings and that if he was to live, his life from this point on was to be spiritual.

He was stunned. Tears filled his eyes as he blurted out that he had been a criminal and only just been released from a very long jail sentence. I suggested he read my first *Modern Seer* book, and as I turned my head to walk away, he asked if I would like to visit him. On turning my head, I noticed three men standing at the bar. The energy was strange and menacing. As I tuned in, quickly but discreetly, I could 'see' that they were not humans, they were demonic. No sooner had the realisation entered my thought field, than one of them, who had very white hair and pale skin, looked straight at me – he could see that I could see him and his two 'friends'. If I had challenged him there and then he may have tried to attack me, but I did not.

Instead, I watched as they vanished. And then I left the premises.

Em seemed pleased with my progress regarding the two tests in the nightclub. I'd advised the man who had just been released from jail, and spoken a spiritual command over his life. I'd also spotted the three lower entities who were watching, but hadn't panicked or overreacted, but instead had stood my ground with faith, and calmly waited for them to disappear. Lower entities can try to interfere with the progress of a person who is emerging out of darkness. Sometimes to try and drag the person back down, at other times just for their own amusement. Em considers them to be like naughty children.

Em went on to say that I had been pushed ahead and would be leading groups of spiritual students, though he cautioned me that even Masters are subject to even higher Masters, all the way up to God. He then added that I must be guarded and guided, and must not commit to any man on earth yet, to just watch and wait.

For many years, much about my past lives had been revealed and shown to me. But, as yet, I didn't know much about the details of my eternal connection with Ray and Em. And, although I had once seen Ray in a vision as part of a group with The Great Prophet Yeshua (Jesus), I was not aware of who the other members were, nor was I privy to know yet that I was a part of The Team! Ray had often laughed and said, "It's teamwork," but he'd never elaborated. Then, one night, I watched in awe as a scene unfolded to enlighten me regarding some of Ray's past lives. First he was shown as a priest wearing long robes, and around his fingers was a clear seal as a sign of holiness. Next, he was shown as a knight on a large horse, and I could see a deep wound in Ray's knee – even in this lifetime he would at times complain about his knee.

Then, in a flash, the scene changed and I was there: I had been captured and was in a line of prisoners with my hands bound, waiting to be put to death. Ray was an official who helped me to escape in that lifetime.

It was not long after this that Ray introduced me to a small group of spiritual aspirants he'd been teaching. Em had said that I would be leading groups of students, and now Ray was passing them on to me. I have a cohort of clients around the world, but my work with my select groups of spiritual students is very different. They are of all nationalities, cultures and backgrounds, with one goal in mind: GOD!

Most of my time was still spent in isolation, living alone with my pets, although I was being encouraged on occasions to attend certain events and accept specific invitations. At one gathering I was instructed to go to, I met the then Prime Minister of England, Gordon Brown. He was very nice and polite, but I felt sad for him as his energy seemed so heavy. Moments later I was introduced to one of the Cabinet Ministers of Serbia, who made a pass at me, which was both surprising and amusing. I of course ignored it, knowing that it had to be a test. That evening, once home alone again, Em said to me, "You have been faithful and good, now enter into the joy of The Divine," adding, "Release your life into the Holy Mind."

The techniques I was being taught were powerful and beautiful, and yielded fantastic results, one of which involved singing. Not just any old song, but specific words. This worked for many things, and so I decided to try and use it for clarity regarding the issue of me living a family life, since confusion around this still assailed me. But the answer that came was, "You will have a companion of God's choice." Followed by, "What is being formed in you must be birthed fully for the next generation." I felt frustration for a few moments, so went into my garden to be in nature. I soon felt soothed, and then apologised, and asked The Divine for forgiveness. Em laughed at me!

Late that night, after my prayers, a wave of energy swept over me and lifted me, and Em said, "The Armour of Light." I felt strong inwardly and secure in the hope that one day the Armour of Light might by given to me, but then Em laughed and said, "You are wearing it!" I sat with him then and meditated. And he said, "Focus on God." Afterwards, he

10

bowed to me with his hands in the prayer position and motioned for me to do the same, saying, "To no longer be burdened with your own will, but to be guided in all things, is both a blessing and a luxury." And after a few moments of gazing silently upon me, he added, "The doorways are open in Eternity." Before sleep, I fell into Divine communion: it felt like love breathing in me. I bowed my head and heard The Divine speak these words, "It is Divine Love."

Ray phoned me the next day to congratulate me and said, "Your neutral feelings about your personal life are because you are responding to a higher calling. You must marry. Just wait for the hand of God.

You've activated a higher law." That evening, after my prayers in the higher realm with Em, I laughed joyfully, staring upwards, and thanked God that I was not under the illusion of love or romantic feelings for any man!

That night I was meditating, cross-legged on the floor with Em, and I heard these words, "Ask The Divine for Grace." I did. And I was told, "Creation needs opposites. The Pure Unmanifest is ONE: non- duality. Nothing created by manifest Beings is perfect or permanent."

Days later I saw Whitey! (One of my guides, who I had not seen for an age.) He was with us in the higher heavenly realm. He levitated as he spoke and said to me, "The result of your efforts is more work. Listen, and look straight ahead. Be a role model." Em smiled but said nothing, as Whitey vanished. When we were alone again, Em said to me, "Be absorbed in the family life that is God's Will." I agreed.

When I next spoke with Ray, he said seriously, "Don't allow people who flatter and praise you to make you proud, or the flattery and praise will take your light. Praise is only for The Divine." And he added gravely, "We beings have created death and the devil from our own thoughts, words and actions." He paused, before saying cautiously, "Some believe that Joseph of Arimathea paid to have Yeshua's body taken from the cross while he was still alive, and that his life continued." This was the first time that Ray had brought up details of his knowledge of Yeshua. I had seen Ray in the group with The Great Prophet in a vision, but Ray would never discuss it. I was desperate to talk with him more about it now, but he said it was for me to find out and know for myself when I was ready. I decided I would put it to prayer and see if Em would enlighten me when the time was right. Ray seemed pleased with my decision, and went on to discuss details about the Great Teacher Padmasambhava.

That night in the higher realm with Em, all of my Guides and Divine helpers appeared and bowed to me. One of them, Teresa the Nun, had lightning in her eyes. I bowed back, and meditated with Em when they had all left. Afterwards, I was curious to know what the lightning in Teresa's eyes had meant, as in the past when I had seen lightning in Em's eyes it had meant trouble. But I was told that I was about to turn a corner. I went off to sleep peacefully shortly after, but was startled by a dream in which Em appeared as an armoured soldier on horseback, wielding a sword high in victory and shouting, "Your strength is in Love." I did not understand his meaning. In my waking state I called upon Em to ask about the dream. I know that dreams have very strong meanings, and that interpretation of dreams is an essential part of esoteric training. Em answered, "You became a partner a while back." That was all he said. I pondered this a lot, and came to the conclusion that I'd become a partner of The Team at some point, although I hadn't any idea when this might have been. I wasn't a million miles from the truth.

The next night, Ray came to me in a dream telling me that Em is much greater than a Master! I called Ray upon waking to ask him the meaning of this, and he said, "There are Masters, and Great Masters. And Em is much greater than these." It then struck me that it was more than a coincidence that I had been guided to name Em as 'The Great One' in the first *Modern Seer* book. And it explained why Em's light had been so bright and overpowering that in the early days I used to shake in his presence. Ray concluded our conversation by saying that Em himself would reveal all when I was ready to know. As I came off the phone, I was called to the higher realm, into an inner hall of worship and told to, "Bow before the Lord of ALL." I did as instructed and stayed in that inner hall of light until I was told, "You are now prepared."

I went about my day assisting clients and students as usual, and then, on going for a shower, these words were shouted at me: "HE has chosen you," and I was called back into the inner hall of light. Once there, a wind began to blow. I bowed down in praise but was raised up as my body was cast off me like it was clothes, and I remained as a pure ball of light; in the air, to praise God! I heard these words spoken to me: "You came into Being to glorify The Divine." From then on, I worshipped The Divine as light! Em soon came and said, "Congratulations! You have won. You bear your psychic scars from the tests, and the scars work as talismans to show the elemental forces and all Beings that you have done your work. When the forces see your talismans – born of your scars – they will know you have paid your karmic debts to the 'evil' and that you are Godly. You are an Initiate!"

A few nights later, the symbolism of female (light), holding hands with male (dark), was revealed to me (in the realms of creation, this level is reached when karmic debt is no longer owed): it equals balance and harmony. Em called out to me to say, "Once the karmic debt is cleared to the 'evil,' a debt may still be owed to The Divine!"

ences with Em from this point on also changed.
...l merge with one another as light, but one day he
...efore my eyes to stand in front of me, smiling and
taki..., hands as he twirled me round, saying, "Be a
Master." He then gestured with his hand to show me a vision:
Em dressed in oriental garb, bowing to me. I bowed back to
him, dressed in gold oriental garb, with black hair piled up on
top of my head. I walked with perfect dignity and poise with
Em beside me. The scene must have been from yet another
previous life, I thought to myself. But Em said, "Everything is
in the Eternal Now," and left. I was told that night that my
life's work is in slavery to The Divine, which is the most
beautiful justice imaginable.

My birthday came around again and I was told that I must
soon move into London. And that my lessons at The Invisible
University were to begin! (See chapter 6 on Mystery Schools.)
Ray called and said with a little laugh, "You are there Cher, if
you go any deeper, your body may burn." He was right about
my body: the pains at times were almost impossible to bear. I
was always advised to pray and breathe through it, but my
physical body was struggling under the weight of the spiritual
alignment taking place in me.

I learned so many things – and indeed still am learning
things – at The Invisible University. One of the first lessons
was on moods in human behaviour. How emotions are not
real, but so strongly illusory that they are dangerous. Are the
invisible powers of emotions ours? Have we created them? Is
it that we use them, or they use us? Em would at times
accompany me on the lessons, but not always. Or not to my
knowledge at this point anyhow. Although on one occasion
Em turned up and staked a tall flag in the ground outside the
building, and then went off again.

After lessons one afternoon, I'd been prompted to burn

my first *Modern Seer* manuscript: the handwritten notes of *The Hidden Secrets of a Modern Seer* book! I did as instructed, of course, but wondered why it was necessary. I was told that this marked the end of my old way of living and that I must welcome in my new Holy Life as an Initiate, which God had given to me. And that I must Bless The Team and get on with the work in London, and that it would soon be time for me to know my position in Eternity!

I then saw myself as a little magician filled with light. As I stood for The Divine with Ray and Em at my side, I was no longer an ant between two giants, but a little magician! "The magician's wand is ours to use," they said, telling me that, "We are in this together."

A mixture in a glass was given to me to drink in The Divine presence, to keep the Law and stay in God's will. I was then enlightened somewhat about Interplanetary Hosts, before The Divine voice spoke to me, saying, "Say your goodbyes to your past and your woes, walk on with your loves at your side, with God as your guide." An azure blue light flashed around me. I was told that I now have the ability to save people by teaching them (those who are ready) the inner-life practices. I was filled with light inside of me, and told that I have a Holy Fire that will burn people in a good way when they come close.

In a session with Em, he told me that total communion with God will come, and that I should enjoy my life. We then prayed together that the *Modern Seer Trilogy* of books will work as The Divine wishes for it to work when people read it. I was shown Ray wearing a long coat made out of tiny mirrors, and it was revealed to me that Ray only seeks comfort in The Divine, as comfort from others is only a distraction.

I told Ray about what had been revealed to me about him and he smiled, and then went on to bring up the 'family life' again. He said this: "Although it will mean you taking a step down in your vibratory rate if you go into married life in the human sense, you will still be doing your service to humanity. And all the effort and credit you have built up in your spiritual account will remain; nothing will be lost." I listened but responded by saying that only God has the solution, so it was not necessary for us to discuss the issue any longer. Ray seemed impressed by my comment, and added, "You are a magician for good only."

It was a beautiful autumn day when next I was promoted. I was called into the inner hall of light, and found myself manifested as my beautiful resplendent Spirit Self, dressed in iridescent white. As I walked forward, responding to the call, I realised I'd stepped on a tiny demon, which quickly ran off to a corner to watch as I bowed before The Divine. I was told to, "Stand up and be counted as one of The Holy Ones."

Em was so happy for me. Then Ray congratulated me, before going on to say that there are Great Beings among us so highly evolved that they can even make bodies for their temporary use to manifest themselves in visible form when they choose. But they rarely reveal their true powers to anyone!

The next day, Ray contacted me telepathically to let me know I should take the train to come and meet him. He then appeared in my clairvoyant field of vision and bowed down, as he said that Em was coming.

Em appeared and I bowed to him too, with Ray, and Em smiled and told me to stand up, putting something clear in my right hand, which went in through the skin. Em said it was to strengthen the weakness in my body. He added that I must shine for The Divine, and disappeared. I then took the train to meet with Ray.

Another day at The Invisible University we were discussing earthly life. The general theme being that nothing about being on earth is normal. We are all totally dependent upon the energy from the fireball in the sky, as well as the invisible forces and gases. We are living, and yet not living. We are trapped and yet not trapped in this spinning world of phases. I studied the Sun's pulses and rays, and came to know that what is termed as The Valley of The Shadow of Death is *this* world. And that using our desire-based free will leads to error in the end, even if things appear to be going well temporarily. Late that night, after meditation with Em, he gave me a supportive hug, and told me that all aspirants and students must learn to use their own inner resources to lift them, so as not to call on Teachers and Divine Helpers too much as it drains them.

Plus, students must build their own inner strength and light. Then Em said, "Don't step down, Cher."

Days later I was told that a holy spell had been put upon me to keep me in Divine will. Em came, and we merged as light and meditated together. As his energy filled my heart centre, I watched him as he snapped a long metal rod over his knee, as if it were a piece of wood. A demon fell head first towards the floor at his side, and, as it struck the ground, he told it that it must work for the Divine. The entity vanished, and Em showed me a square sandstone on the floor, with a few holes in the top. He said, "It's an immovable foundation for the future, but it's not perfect!" He waited as I studied the sandstone before adding, "The Masters don't hear everything from the Cosmos, they just hear what they need to hear."

Em took me to walk with him by a calm pool of water. As we went on together, a big black man, a chief with a headdress on, came and stood in front of us. Staring into my eyes, the chief soon stepped aside so that I could see Ray's Teacher, SEG, behind him in a small dwelling. He appeared to be in meditation but upside down! He had smoke billowing around him, and he explained that the smoke was from burning a small green herb from the mountains, and that within the smoke one can see many things. He added that he had lived on the family path and had more than one child, but that only his daughter was highly gifted. It was revealed that Ray had met his teacher, SEG, when he was studying for a degree but had suffered a breakdown due to the psychic attacks he had been experiencing since a young boy. As a toddler, he had been subjected to lower entities sitting on him, pulling his hair, and at one point had been attacked and hit in the solar plexus so severely that the bouts of pain from it continued until he grew into a young man. I was told that Ray had asked one day in prayer for the pain from his psychic attack to be released from him, and was answered, "Who do you wish to carry it instead?" He realised that it was a part of his own karma, and thus his cross to carry! As more was relayed about Ray to me, I saw a holy link that emanated from him and me, which spread out and linked around the entire world, and fused in holy light at the centre.

When one is called to the Spiritual Path, one is expected to take either the family path or the celibate path, depending upon one's destiny within The Divine Plan. Either way, one is not supposed to experiment with romantic relationships. The following night, I was instructed to perform a prayer ritual using specific incense, herbs, and flowers. As I performed the ritual, I was called up to the inner hall of light; and as I my made my way, there were Angels standing to my left and right, watching me as I walked forward to worship The Divine. Soon after, Em stepped forward and placed a holy kiss on my forehead, before telling me to rest.

I gave a spiritual gift of thanks to Ray, when I saw him a few days later: it resembled a silvery-gold- like substance. He was delighted, and said to me, "The Masters always smile, because they do not focus on what is transient in this world,

18

they focus on the Eternal!" And later, when I was at home, the picture of me in Greece, where my guide HL had first manifested himself to me on the beach, had moved. In prayer that evening, I was told that I can create Blessings!

As I lay in bed, unable to fall asleep, I was called to get up and go to the window. It was late, and pitch dark outside. I had only been standing there for a few moments when from within an overwhelming power emerged, flinging open the window with great force! A mighty wind began to blow and my arms were pushed outstretched into the night sky, as I heard my voice being 'used' to call out, "God's will be done in the Heavens and on Earth." Moments later the wind calmed, and I regained composure. A white mist floated in the air, the azure light flashed around me, and I heard Em say, "Congratulations."

The next morning I had a flash vision of myself standing at Ray's graveside in years to come. And I saw Ray as a purple gem psychically as I was told that he is a 'Universal Treasure.' During my prayers in the evening, I heard The Divine speak to me, "When you merge with the Light, that is ME." In the early hours, as I became light to worship The Divine, my light merged with the light inside the inner hall. I was suddenly back in my body, sitting opposite Em, who said, very intently, to focus upon him, gesturing with his hands to direct my eyes towards his, and showering me with a light substance. He slowly vanished from view as he continued to shower me with the substance, and then showed me a wedding ceremony. The scene faded as Em told me to rest, and placed a holy kiss on my forehead with his finger.

Later that week, a lady that I help had called me to say, "I know that you have powers to change things, why don't you change things for me?" This happened often but not in quite so bold a fashion. I explained that unless it is sanctioned for me to do such things, to change the course of events in someone's life or intervene in their karma, I cannot, no matter who they are or how much they may feel they deserve it. At the close of my meditation that evening, I saw a huge gold Buddha statue. And after praying, I merged with The Divine Light of God, as pure light! Ray called me afterwards to say, "I am no longer your Teacher, Cher. You are my Teacher. We are assisting each other. God is about to breathe on you, I am very happy for you!"

Days later The Divine spoke to me again, saying, "Cleanse people and bring them to ME." I was told to sprinkle the Holy Ash, and go to the city and lead the excellent exemplary life of harmlessness. At midnight, my guide HL appeared. He had five swords for fingers on his hand, and said, "You are going to be a Master; you are at the gates." And in a flash I was in a room with Em and HL, who watched me as I left the room to walk through a passageway alone. I saw a closed iron gate as I walked on, which lower entities were trapped behind: they were crying and screaming and trying to force their way through, but the gate was firmly shut! I was moved by their cries but felt very strong and just walked on, without hesitation, through another iron gate, which was open for me just up ahead. Once through it, I was in The Divine presence and my light merged with the Divine Light!

When next I was with Em, a sword came to us and hovered in mid-air. I was told, "It's your sword to wield and use." And I took it in both hands and swirled it in the air. Late that night, I was back in the room with HL and Em, who bowed to me upon my arrival. As I bowed back to them, a woman with an air of great confidence suddenly appeared at HL's side. She had her hair pulled back in a bun, and was young-looking. She smiled at me. And then a tall man with grey hair entered the room, tipped his hat to greet me, and quickly said, "Goodbye," before leaving. I came to realise that these were some of the members of The 'hidden' Team. Em motioned for us to leave together. Outside, we stood and looked across the strong iron bridge that stretched out before us into the distance. Em said, "No one can reach us or join us unless first they battle their way across the iron bridge, as you have done, to be safely with us."

A few weeks later, I took a holiday to visit friends in America. I continued with my prayers and meditations on the trip. On arriving home, feeling jet-lagged, I decided I needed to go and rest in bed. As I began to fall asleep, I kept seeing very bright flashes of blue light. The next thing I knew, Em was waking me up, saying, "We must pray together." We did, and afterwards I felt so tired that I tried to lie down and rest again, but Em gently said, "You cannot sleep now, we need to talk." I said that I was too tired, and asked what we needed to talk about right now, and he replied, "We must talk of love,", and held my hand, to show me a ring on my finger. I looked down at it, and then looked at him and said, "I cannot focus on this now." He looked a little sad but let it go, and then left. I had thought this was to be yet another discussion about me leading a family life, and I just couldn't focus on such things in my half asleep, jet-lagged state.

When I woke up, The Divine spoke to me, saying, "Bring ME an offering." I was instructed to gather a specific herb, particular flowers, sprigs of wood, as well as certain petals. I was told that anyone who says they know everything and have all the answers, or who claim to be God – including religious leaders and spiritual teachers – is under an illusion of the ego and is serving Satan (perhaps without even knowing it)! "Even the Angels, The Great Ones and The Prophets are not God," Em came and said as I kneeled to pray.

He had a look of indifference as he instructed me to be in

silence, and I did so, as pure light. He told me that, "The Lord loves and protects you," and I responded by saying that I loved God, and I loved him. Em touched the palms of my hands and said, "God will put the Blessings of life and death in your hands."

The next day, Em showed me places where he had hidden things in the earth, and the day after that he showed me where he was meditating, sitting on a spot where he had hidden things yesterday! We discussed the elemental forces, and, as an exercise, I prayed for nicer weather as it was a dull, cloudy day: I saw little nature spirits run forward joyfully as they moved clouds to show forth the Sun, and then they made a flower bloom instantly in front of us!

A few days later, Em and I merged and entered the inner hall of light to pray. There it was revealed to us that Ray is following the path of Christhood. I was told to be still and focus, while The Holy Spirit bestowed the 'Seeds of Love' upon me. As the energy glided through me, I was informed that The Holy Spirit is female!

I spoke with Ray sometime later, and of course, he knew of my experiences, and said, "Brilliant!" He went on to say, "On the Path, some may seek you to rob you of your light. Choose very wisely who you visit and allow to be in your aura, and always check with your 'inner voice' first!" After prayers that evening, as I merged with The Divine Light, my light became invisible!

Em taught me a new meditation technique, which involved smiling. During the session, we had been meditating and smiling with our eyes closed – it was hard not to giggle actually – when Em suddenly opened one eye and said, "I am keeping an eye on you, and I am with you always!" It was so joyful, and afterwards he explained that there is a reason why there are so many statues of the smiling Buddha.

In my next conversation with Ray, he said, "Hold on to Em's hand tightly, you are taking on a lot of work." That night, as I prayed to God, Em appeared and said, "It is clear that you are in love with God." He bowed to me, and I bowed back.

But the following day I heard these words: "The battle continues ... to win your love." I was confused.

Em prompted me to open my hands, then came and held them in his. We kneeled to pray together, and afterwards I was given an instruction regarding my work for human redemption. Em said, "There is one more thing ... a ring!" and placed a ring on a finger of my right hand. I was told to lay myself bare before The Divine. As I asked for forgiveness and to be as God would have me be, my light became invisible as I merged with The Divine Light, and I heard the words, "Shh, just give yourself to ME. You are so close to The Temple of marriage ... Commit, and you will be free."

Each time the issue of marriage and family life came up it unnerved me. It did not seem or feel quite right somehow. Ray had said to me recently that The Divine is jealous. Not in the human sense, but that God must choose who is to live on the family path and who is to live on the celibate path. That night I prayed again for guidance. I soon merged with The Divine Light, and as my light became invisible, and I was held in the Bliss, The Divine blew the Godly essence in me! And I heard these words: "I live in you now," followed by, "Work, love, and live for ME."

CHAPTER 2
LIGHTNING STRIKES

Em appeared at my bedside to give me a message: "The Lord has a Blessing for you". It was a dark and stormy night and I could hear the sea roaring outside. My hand had begun hurting and had started to swell. Em went on, "Power proceeds from you and through you," and then disappeared. My throbbing hand was distracting me, but suddenly an impulse shot through me and I was compelled to get up and run to my conservatory downstairs. The same overwhelming power that I had experienced a couple of months back emerged again, flinging open the glass conservatory doors with great force! The storm was still raging outside, and flashes of lightning appeared over the sea. My hands were suddenly forced outstretched into the night sky, as a crack of lightning struck my fingers and shockwaves rippled through my hands. As I sat on the ground, I could see waves of light flowing up my fingers, and could no longer move my hands or my wrists properly. As I made my way back up to bed, I heard these words: "The powers to Bless and to Curse."

I wish to add here that from childhood many strange things, both good and bad, have happened to people who came into contact with me (see *The Hidden Secrets of a Modern Seer* book for details). But, after the experience on the night that the lightning touched my hands, things became much more intense. I also wish to explain that these 'powers' that flow through me are not mine: they are part of a higher Spiritual Law. It is neither my decision nor my doing, but what happens to people when they meet me or speak with me is to do with their karma being quickened and played out, and, if you will, blessed or judged by the powers that be. The Divine revealed to me that as a worker for The Divine Plan, it is a part of my duty to have certain blessings, commands and judgments flow through me. Not from me, but through me. What I reveal regarding examples of events may seem shocking to you the reader: I assure you, when these instances take place they are just as shocking to me. I hasten to add that on occasions I have got on my knees to plead and pray to God that no harm may come to someone who has angered or annoyed me, or spoken blasphemously in my presence, as often when people do so, they suffer tragic consequences. Conversely, many miraculous blessings have manifested through me for people, regardless of whether or not I may feel they are worthy or deserving. It is God's Will, not mine. (Please see the Case Studies chapter for examples.)

The pain I experienced after the lightning strike was indescribable. So agonising was it one day that I had to crawl from the bedroom to the top of the stairs, using my elbows for support and sliding down the stairs on my bottom as I was in too much pain to stand up. It was at this point that one of my relatives came to put food through the cat flap for me, as I was unable to stand up to open the front door, let alone go out food shopping. Em was performing healing rituals with me, and Ray had called to advise me on specific items to ease the pain, but it did not shift entirely. When I was able to get out and drive my car again, I went again to see medical specialists (one at the hospital, and one on Harley Street). I could not, of course, explain in any way to the experts what was happening to me, but I had many tests, and listened to the medical advisers' words, only to be told when the test results came in that I was very slightly anaemic, and that the swelling in my fingers and hands had caused my wrists to fuse. To this day, I have very little movement in my wrists, although much healing has taken place in my hands.

Another New Year had begun and I could feel that this would be a significant one. Em came, and painted my face and gave me an elixir in a murky looking glass to drink, as he danced around me saying that he was preparing me for the next phase. This could only mean one thing: the experimental tests of romance again!

Days later, I received multiple invitations to attend gatherings, and also had contact from some of my ex-suitors and other interested men. I was encouraged to 'as a spy' have very brief conversations with potential candidates but not to indulge or engage with anyone intimately. Em reminded me that my marriage was the goal, and Ray called to say, "You are a Mystic, you have come into this incarnation with this orientation, and you are ahead of many. You must continue with your work, helping your students, and you may travel. The Masters are waiting for you to decide on your marriage."

I intended to do as instructed, bearing in mind that I knew all too well that The Masters could shift things at any time if they are sanctioned to by The Divine, and that everything is a test! And I began to socialise again, although the enthusiasm was not there as it was in the past, and, instead of excitement, I felt drained and disappointed by the men I spent time with. My love for God was strong, and although I wanted to 'manifest' a family life to please God, if it was Divine Will, something still seemed amiss regarding this aim. I came home from a gathering one evening and was so uplifted in the presence of The Divine, that I was compelled to write a poem for God. I will share a small part of it with you here:

Tenderness trembled as passion applauded,
In the face of Love's embrace.
The darkness heaved to right itself,
In the Light of True Love's Grace.

CHAPTER 3
MY LAST EXPERIMENT

I began travelling again, which I enjoy immensely, and I made sure that I spent time with the potential candidates as instructed, two of whom, for the time being, were an American man and an Englishman. These were the main two, along with three others I was being encouraged to 'entertain in discussions' and spend brief periods of time with, due to the fact that they all had a spiritual turn of mind.

Ray had called late one night to say that I must pray very hard as a step had to be taken soon, and Em had warned me that I must not go out of God's Will again. This was a lot of pressure, and quite honestly, I did not enjoy my discussions with the American, as he was very patriarchal and aggressive in his approach. Neither did I enjoy my talks with the Englishman very much, as he was quite prideful, and somewhat snobbish.

It was then revealed to me that the density of the maya of this dimension had tricked me into the relationships I had experimented with in my youth in this lifetime. I had memories played back before my eyes of my experiments with the famous male models, the famous actor, and the musician. I felt deep remorse. I was told that if I was to come into incarnation again, due to maya being so heavy in this realm I might even be tricked again, albeit temporarily!

I turned to Em for guidance, but he kept saying that I must choose, and do God's Will. I also turned to Ray to discuss this issue yet again, but he just kept saying that for now I would lead the celibate ascetic path, but that I must live my family life! The frustration and confusion was at times

27

enraging.

One morning, one of my students emailed me to say that a wonderful dream had been revealed to them about my future work and personal life. It was uplifting, and I was grateful that at times my students would 'tune in' to assist me too, although this was very rare!

It was after this that Em came to say, "It is sad that love is so temporary in this world – I speak of romantic love particularly – but you can continue your discussions with the American, the Englishman and the three others, and see! Ultimately though, your work must take priority, and you must spread light all over the world." He covered me with a white material and told me to pray, and also to fast for the next three days.

As time went on, the American became impatient, and even went as far as to lose his temper and say that he 'felt' there was some kind of a conspiracy going on to keep us apart. There was of course, although not in the sense that he would understand. But I was not at liberty to reveal the secrets of this 'test' I was enduring.

I also had three proposals of marriage around this time, two of which were by phone! The first was from a male friend whom I had known for many years; a sweet and brilliantly clever man, whom I love very much as a friend. He called me one afternoon, out of the blue, as he sat in the Charlotte Street Hotel in London. His monologue went something like this: "No chap is going to be good enough, so I am asking you to marry me, as I love you, and I know that we get along tremendously. What do you say?" I was stunned, and after a few moments silence, laughed, then went on to say how much I loved him as a friend and that as much as I appreciated his offer, we would be best off as friends for life. And I reminded him of how odd I can be at times, and that he would find my spending so much of my time in the other realms of existence frustrating. He laughed and agreed, and that was the end of that!

The second marriage proposal came from a highly distinguished barrister friend of mine. His phone call came on a day when I had taken to my bed due to exhaustion. He had called to say that after not having seen me for so many months he missed our conversations terribly, and thought it silly that I would not agree to just marry him and live happily together with our pets. He had been a bachelor up to this point, and had not as yet ever married either, despite certain ladies having been very much 'in love' with him, and having stayed in relationships with him in the hope that he might propose marriage one day. I consider this man to be one of my most trusted male friends, but it had not been sanctioned for me to consider him as a potential candidate. And in fact I was instructed to encourage him to marry someone else, which he eventually did!

Then, to add a little extra spice into the mix, Ray called me one day to say that someone new would be coming into the picture. I was not certain if I felt relieved or outraged: the tests just kept on coming, and I just had to keep on going. A few nights later, Em came and told me to light a candle in my heart for the men that were vying for my hand in marriage, and to keep aiming for God's Will. Then the biggest of the tests came. The musician I had been in love with in the past got back in touch. My feelings for him were ignited again the moment I received his message saying that he still loved me as much as ever, missed me and my pets, and wanted to know if he could come back. I was devastated.

A few days later, when I was travelling, I happened to bump into the musician: he took my hand, and – as tears filled his eyes – asked if he could come home with me, expressing his wish for us to marry and have a child together. In my flustered state, I managed to ignore his request, and instead suggested that he call me. Needless to say, I went home alone.

After Ray's message of 'someone new' coming, I had not been expecting to meet or hear from my old flame. My feelings for him rose like a phoenix from the ashes, and I could feel my strength waning. But I was not giving up. I would not be accepting anyone unless it was God's Will.

I allowed the days to pass, and did nothing in relation to the tests regarding the men. Then, late one afternoon, after assisting clients and students by phone, one of my beloved cats – my boy! – collapsed in a heap at my feet. I gasped in horror as his body lay limp on the floor in front of me, his eyes half-closed. I wondered if he might have died on the spot. In a panic, I ran to gather some sacred items to perform a ritual to revive him. I prayed on my knees to God as I carried out the ceremony, and after some time his eyes began to flicker. Suddenly he jumped up, full of life and vigour! The tears streamed down my face as I thanked God for the Blessing. My boy was elderly, but so precious to me: I could not bear to lose him just yet.

A few days later, I was prompted to cut up small pieces of white paper, and write the names of each of 'the potential candidates' on them before placing them under my pillow – or more accurately, inside my pillowcase – so I could sleep over them. I had been told that The Masters would not choose for me, that I must choose God's Will. And then I heard these words: "Yeshua loves you."

On waking the next morning, I discovered three of the names from inside my pillowcase (one of them the American's), lying on the floor on the other side of the bedroom. I was told to discard them.

Ray and I discussed my latest experiences, and he seemed

30

pleased but just said, "You are in tune with the folk spirit of England, and must move into London soon." Much was revealed about particular cities and countries around the world, and the specific places that are spiritual hubs for The Masters and Teachers. Ray smiled as he relayed to me that his Teacher, SEG, many years ago had revealed to him that England is the spiritual and mystical centre of the world! Later that week I met up with Ray for dinner, after agreeing to a rare face-to-face session with a television celebrity. (The majority of my work was now by phone and Skype.)

Next, Em was to warn me to not go too far away – to not take any further trips abroad for a time, but just to stay put and complete this phase. He went on, "The winds of change come again." The next night, the piece of paper with the musician's name on fell from my pillowcase, and I was told to discard it and not engage with him again. Afterwards, I prayed opposite Em, and disappeared as I worshipped in the presence of God.

Some time later, when I met up with the Englishman again to talk, he was arrogant and rude, and did not treat me well, and I received a prompting to tear up the piece of paper under my pillow that had his name on. Within a couple of weeks, what he had described to me as his 'worst nightmare' happened to him. His piece of paper had been the last one. This only left the 'someone new' for me to meet, who I'd been told about.

I asked Em and Ray why I had needed to go through with the 'names on white paper' exercise, and spend time in discussions with those potential candidates. It was explained to me that God gives deserving people opportunities, and then sees what those people will do with them. The men in question had all been given chances, but were apparently not ready to live the life that I am living, and thus they had to be left behind.

The following weekend I was invited to a gathering. Amongst the guests were a certain Prince and his sister, the Princess. The Prince – a bachelor – seemed to like me and although he seemed somewhat shy, he had a gentleness about him which I admired. After managing to have a conversation amidst the crowd, I soon wished him and the other guests well, and left.

The next day I was prompted to go for lunch with a group of people in London. It was at this very lunch that I would see the gentleman who would become my 'last experiment'. We had chatted very briefly at the table, and although we'd only spoken for a few minutes, he'd made me laugh very much. And he was incredibly polite, with excellent manners. In fact, he reminded me that we had met once before, just for a few seconds, at a party years ago. After lunch, I said my goodbyes to the group, and made my way home.

I felt lifted and inspired at the end of what had been a lovely weekend. That is, until I prayed that night. As I invisibly worshipped in The Divine presence, and was giving thanks, The Divine spoke these words to me: "Give your boy to ME, and I will return him to you in another form." I sobbed and pleaded for my boy to live. The Divine promised to give him to me again – in this life – but I begged to be allowed to keep him for a while longer now. Then silence. I turned to my beloved boy, who was gently purring by me, and I kissed him, before running to gather the sacred items to perform a ritual to prolong his life!

As I leaned over my boy and began the preparations for the ceremony, the phone rang. I would have ignored it but it kept on ringing: it was Ray! He said, "Cher, what are you doing? You cannot go against the will of God. You must not perform this ritual, for you know if you do, it will work. And God has asked you to return your boy! So you must." He

32

reminded me that the Great Teacher Paramahansa Yogananda had been in a similar situation with his pet deer. I was so distraught as I came off the phone that I could hardly breathe.

I cannot describe the battle that went on within me, and the strength that it took for me to not perform that ritual. The next morning I gave my beloved boy back to The Divine. Hours later, Em appeared, holding my boy in his arms! I called out to God as Em stood stroking my beloved boy, and I declared that I would vouch for my boy, and would myself pay off any karmic debt that he had left. Vicarious atonement was sanctioned, and I was assured that my boy's place with The Divine was secure. And also assured that he would be returning to me again soon.

Later that evening I went into Em's abode, and saw my boy laying by the fire. He miaowed as I came close to comfort him. I lit a candle and placed it by him, telling him that I will always be with him, and love him forever. Em told me that my boy would be looked after by him, until he is returned to me again, and said, "God is waiting for an answer." I replied, "An answer to what?" And Em responded, "Will you agree to marry?" I thought it a ridiculous question, requiring no answer, since I believed I was already fully responding and living my life in accordance with God's Will.

The next day, I had called Ray to thank him for having stopped me from performing the ritual for my boy. He was as humble as ever, and said that he was always happy to assist a fellow pilgrim, adding, "Pray for the stability of your emotions." We had a very interesting discussion about the great Teacher Nagarjuna, and his chief disciple, after which I tried my best to go off to sleep. But I became filled with anger that I had been asked to give my boy back to God. Tears flowed as I prayed for forgiveness in the hope of releasing the rage, and I heard these words: "All argue with God at times.

Even the Great Prophet Yeshua, when he was on the cross!"

A few days passed, and I received another invitation: this time, to dine with the Prince, and his sister the Princess, along with two dear old friends of mine. We enjoyed an evening of sparkling conversation, during which time it came to light that the Prince loved dogs, and that his sister was very interested in spirituality! After dinner, the Prince was keen to take a stroll so that we could talk. Which we did. He was gentle and somewhat shy in his manner, and I admired the fact that he was not showy or snobbish in any way – and it amused me greatly when he had said that he liked trains! He went on to reveal some details regarding his private residences as we continued to walk slowly along. Eventually, we exchanged numbers.

I was not expecting anything to come of my connection with the Prince. I know only too well that things can be switched at any time, and that all things – especially romantic relationships – are a test! The following week, as I prayed, I was called to 'come home.' As I heard the words echo from The Divine Source, I could see myself sitting in my own heart centre. Em stood by and watched as my guide Whitey revealed that they, along with other members of The Team, were supporting me. They rolled me as they wrapped me from head to foot in a cloth, and said, "God needs you to fulfil your destiny". Exasperated, I replied, "What is it that I am meant to do? The training and tests have gone on for years. Please just tell me what it is that is expected of me." Em said, "You made a promise," then instructed me to repeat a certain prayer three times. Frustrated and exhausted, I went to bed. I awoke with pains in my head. I felt angry, and said to God, "I have prayed, and obeyed, and still I am confused. Please grant me the strength to go on and do your will, come what may. But let me have clarity." I needed to know what the promise was that I had made. The answer came: "The promise will be made clear, Blessed One of God. All is well."

After I'd worked with my students, Em came to tell me to be ready at the same time tomorrow. And also to not listen to the requests that were coming from the potential candidates I had left behind. Some of them were still trying to make frequent contact, most of which I was ignoring. I had wished them well, and made my excuses by indicating to them that I had to focus on my spiritual life, which is true!

Sure enough, I was ready at the appointed time the following day. Em told me to close my eyes, and hold out my hands. I did so, and felt something being poured into my palms. When I was told to look, I saw light in one hand and liquid gold in the other, and Em told me to merge the two together. When I'd completed the exercise, he said he was pleased with my ability to use and work with the powers, and congratulated me on allowing them to flow through me, rather than from me as part of my own free will.

Hence, my being given this new Blessing and responsibility today!

Before sleep, I went within to worship The Divine. During my blissful at-one-ment, The Divine voice spoke these words to me gently, "You have stolen from me." A sobbing feeling welled in my being, as my essence replied softly, "Stolen what?" And after a few moments of silence, The Divine uttered the following words: "Time. You have stolen time from ME. The time each Being is given is a Blessing to serve and glorify The Divine. Each moment wasted out of God's Will is time stolen. The Divine Plan is delayed with every second not spent in fulfilling one's Divine purpose." I was deeply sorry. And vowed to spend the rest of my incarnation in fulfilling God's Will on earth!

Em encouraged me to go and meet up with Ray, as he had

someone he wished for him to introduce me to. I called Ray, who laughed and said, "Yes, I do actually. Come in to London, and I will make the arrangements for the meeting." The person they wanted me to meet was a Shaolin Monk! Ray set up a time, and we arrived at the front door of a period building in London. The Monk smiled and nodded as he uttered in very broken English that he did not speak the language well. He was only visiting England with his Master. During the afternoon, it was explained that the Monk had been in the Temple since he was six years old, and had been raised as a strict vegetarian, and of course was living on the celibate path. The Monk then offered to perform some healing, if I would like. I agreed, and sat in a little room with him as he smiled and pulled up the sleeves of his robes. To my amazement, when he touched my elbow it went in to a spasm, so much so that my body contorted and began twisting round. The Monk smiled and said not to worry. I asked to look at his hands as he touched me again: there were electric sparks coming from his fingers! He touched me again, and my upper body went into shock. He moved his electric fingers around my collarbone, and motioned to me that it had been broken. I assented with my eyes, as I was finding it hard to move my mouth to speak. As he continued, he mentioned that I should 'move inland,' to which I nodded as much as I was able. He bowed to me at the close of the healing session, after saying that he had a sword too, but different to mine!

Ray had waited for me outside, and afterwards, we went to have tea at the National Gallery to discuss this afternoon's events. As we sat in the cafe in that beautiful building, I felt tears welling in my eyes. Ray blinked as he frowned at me: I was supposed to be in control of my emotions. I apologised, and explained that I had overwhelming feelings of sadness: that I deeply wished I had lived a celibate life, and never

36

experimented with romantic relationships at all! Ray smiled and said, "Well, perhaps the Monk may wonder if he could have led the family path, after meeting you today. It is human to wonder. Who knows, The Masters may have shifted you out of the need to marry. But ultimately, it must be God's choice."

When I got home to my lovely pets, I began looking up Monasteries and Nunneries online. The feeling was so strong that I had made a terrible mistake in not having led a fully celibate life. I called on Em later that evening, and he arrived with a flower! As he gave it to me, he blew on the petals and said, "You're magical." Then told me to watch, as he sat with me after placing my beloved boy in my lap. I asked Em if I were meant to live in a Monastery or a Nunnery, as I stroked my boy. He smiled and replied, "God does not wish for you to live in a Nunnery or a Monastery. God wishes for your life to be a message for ALL, not just the few." We merged together as our light disappeared, to worship in The Divine presence.

The next day, my guide Whitey showed up wafting smoke around me. Em watched as Whitey continued to swirl the mist within my space. I asked what this was for, and Whitey said, "We know you can't continue like this." Em interjected, and said, "Get ready for the 'someone new' and move on." I saw a flash vision of the gentleman I had spoken with briefly at the lunch a couple of months back. This period was to be one of the most confusing and perplexing that I had experienced thus far, and that's saying something!

Henceforth, I will be referring to the gentleman in question as Lex. He was, as I mentioned earlier, funny and incredibly polite, with excellent manners. But he was not perfect. In fact, on the first weekend that I had planned to meet up with him alone, for lunch, Em had said gravely, "He has three dark forces within him to fight: selfishness, sexual appetite, and avarice." These lower-self issues sounded pretty serious to me, although not as serious as the fact that he was not a vegetarian. He was, though – thank goodness – an animal lover. And he was non-violent. If I recall correctly, he had once said to me that he found violence to be unacceptable and abhorrent, which was a great relief.

During the months that I spent giving Lex the chance to polish up, as Ray would put it, I was besieged by horrid dreams. Mostly about Lex's lower self, as well as the human condition, and how far from living in Divine Will – and fulfilling The Divine Plan – humanity was. As we got to know each other better and discussed spirituality, I came to find him charming, but somewhat non-committal in terms of his faith in a higher power, or, to be precise, God. As he came to witness some of the phenomena that at times would happen around me, he also became somewhat fearful. Anyhow, for whatever reason the forces had in mind for us to experiment with being together. I had grown fond of him despite the aforementioned issues.

I continued my lessons and practices with Em, and was keen to know, as always, his thoughts on things, especially now that I was giving Lex some of my time. Em did not say too much, but I noticed that his look and tone of voice had become much more serious. And on one occasion he said, "Do the work with Lex, and let's see if you want him," which confused me a lot. And when I updated Ray over dinner, he frowned and hardly looked up from his food, then said, as he glanced at me briefly, "Supposing I were to step down now, and get involved with a person romantically. It would be like hurling myself into a pit of excrement – of my own volition – and who would get me out?" Stunned at his statement, I quickly replied, "I have been told that I must get on with my family life. And if it is God's Will, I will do just that." Ray nodded and just said, "Let's see." He stared into space for a protracted period of time, and then said, "Shall we go?" Things went on like this for months, and in my anger and frustration one day, I shouted at Em. He told me to be careful, or I may end up eating humble pie. After which, I got him flowers, to show him how sorry I was.

Lex had revealed to me that he had been celibate for the last three years or so, which is a long time for a young man. I was impressed. And, during our discussion over lunch about asceticism, he had said, "How did I get to deserve you? Perhaps because I have been saving myself for you?" I was surprised at his words, but was pretty sure that what he had stated was true!

Em had shown me the ring again and said, "Will you go ahead with marriage?" I replied that if it was God's Will I would. That night I had the most hideous nightmare: I was running in the dark, screaming that I hated God. Ray was there, telling me to burn all the books in my library. I woke up in a sweat and cried out to God, "How is it that the Saints rejoice in your will, yet I am now filled with confusion? Where are my ecstatic moments with YOU?" And as my tears flowed, a beautiful and blissful essence soothed my soul.

A few days later, Em came to deliver a message, saying, "Lex is afraid of you, and afraid to commit. But, if he is to have his chance with you he must cross the rubicon and commit fully!" Then he vanished. And Whitey appeared, saying, "Em wants you back in his camp." But before I could start shouting at Whitey to explain what he meant, he too vanished. I ran into the inner realms to search for Em, calling out to him, but he did not come back: he just shouted to me, "We are a Team. Before you were born, you were destined for the prophetic work!"

A few weeks went by, and the ring Em had kept mentioning to me manifested – except that it didn't look like the ring that Em had shown me! Lex could tell that I seemed confused when I opened the box (or perhaps he thought I didn't like the ring), but my reaction was purely owing to the fact that it wasn't the ring I'd been shown. Also, Lex had not proposed: the ring was a gift, not an engagement ring – engagement rings come with proposals. The day that Lex gave me the ring, Em had come to say, "The body does not need meat, and God requires self-sacrifice." I got on my knees to pray, but Em said sternly, "Why go on your knees if you have not sinned? Sit up and pray properly." After I'd prayed, Em stood over me and placed a droplet of blood on my forehead. Then he crushed, sprinkled, and blew something over me, saying, "You are marked, and all the worlds will salute you, by God's Holy Power. Now fulfil your mission, and let's get on with the work."

I had spent many hours in conversations with Lex, explaining as much as I was prompted to about the Spiritual Laws and the destiny of humanity. Yet still, he had not given up eating meat. Having said that, in fairness to him, he usually ate vegetarian food when he was with me. But of late he had made less of an effort than formerly, and had started to sometimes order fish when we ate together. Then one morning, when we had met for breakfast, he ate bacon in front of me. As the grease slid around his plate and the remnants of flesh smeared his mouth, I felt sickened and disgusted. Plus, he had been raised in the Jewish faith. And in the Jewish faith, one is not supposed to eat meat from pigs. I was deeply disturbed by his behaviour, and was sure this was why Em had said when I last saw him that, "The body does not need meat, and God requires self-sacrifice." His message was not intended for me: I knew full well about this aspect of living harmlessly.

It was almost Christmas time again, and Em came dressed

40

in a fantastic theatrical attire, with a top hat and tails, leaning on his sword like it was a cane, and said to me, "You must go with Ray, and find a place to move to in London." Then with a little dance, he added, "There will be games, films, songs, and more books!"

During a telephone conversation with my Grandmother one evening, as we discussed my moving in to London, the idea of doing a little research into our family tree came about. This was born out of the fact that Ray had said to me recently, "You have an aristocratic gloss on your life, Cher." I certainly didn't feel terribly aristocratic, but decided it would be worth chatting with my only senior relative left alive, to see what may be discovered about our ancestors. I had always known that we had English, Scottish and French lineage, but not too much about the details. My Grandmother and I enjoyed many laughs as she shared stories regarding some of our family members. Especially in relation to her Great Uncle Robert who had refused to have sex and consummate his marriage with his wife, as he did not wish to lose his power to levitate! My Grandmother relayed her childhood memories of her having gone to stay with Uncle Robert, who had a very large house but chose to live by himself in his outhouses, by candlelight, as his lonely wife roamed the halls of their grand home alone. It also came to light that our relative Viscount Horne, who was the Chancellor of the Exchequer, was quite a character: a ladies man and staunch bachelor who refused to marry or have children. Suffice it to say, that there have been many interesting characters in our family line.

Ray laughed and said, "You see, I told you!" when I revealed some of the private details my Grandmother had spoken of about my lineage. And then he added, "You are noble Cher, and your being noble in the higher spiritual echelons is recognised too!" I turned our conversation to the pain in my body, and Ray curtly said, "Do you want someone else to carry the pain for you?" Of course I didn't, so the topic was ended there.

The New Year ushered in an energy of change and new beginnings. I had mentioned discreetly to a couple of my trusted friends that I would soon be moving into London. We had an intimate little leaving party, and by February my beloved pets and I had moved. Em had come one evening, calling me his 'White Rose' and relaying to me that the number of my students would be increasing. He showed me opening the front door to a period house in London, but it was not the period property I'd just moved into. Em came in close and spoke softly, saying, "You must not reveal what I tell you in secret from now on, even if Ray wishes to discuss everything with you. There will be things that will be hidden from him too. And you've no need to tell him. We, 'The Team', will be holding meetings and collaborating. God's Will and work must be done." Some members of The Team appeared, and bowed to Em, who went on, "You are a spy between the worlds, and a steward on earth."

More magazines were running articles on my first book, *The Hidden Secrets of a Modern Seer*, and Em came to say that it was just the beginning, and God would be guiding and blessing our projects as they were a part of The Divine Plan. He showed me a vision of when we were together as warriors in a life before. And he said, "Always set aside time for me," which I do. He shouted, "Tune in!" and as I did, a lump of malleable gold was placed in my hands. Em said to me, "You can do with it whatever you wish!" It moved like a liquid. He added, "You can use little drops or pieces of it. You can love the whole world with it, or you can throw it like a grenade!" I prayed with the gold substance in my hands, and then gave it all up to God. I felt bliss and euphoria. Em was pleased I had passed this test, and said to me, "You can use the gold from now on if you wish, as you are creating it within you!"

I hadn't travelled since Em had instructed me to not go too far for a time, and I hoped I might be able to take trips again soon, but Em said, "You will have to wait!" He then revealed a scene in which he was spreading white rose petals outside of the period house in London he had shown me entering before. That evening, I met with an old friend of mine, Reg, who had trained with Ronald Beesley and Krishnamurti for ten years. He's an extraordinarily interesting chap, and I enjoyed our mirthful conversations immensely.

Valentine's Day came around, and Lex had given me a red heart from Tiffany's! And taken me for dinner at a vegetarian restaurant in Soho. Before prayers that night, Em came to say that I'd be disappointed in Lex. I wish to mention here, that Saint Valentine (Valentinus), a third century Roman, Bishop and Martyr, was put in prison, tortured, beaten with clubs, and eventually beheaded on February 14th for refusing to renounce his Faith. Which really has nothing to do with human romantic love, and everything to do with love of God. Late that night, as I focused on The Divine, I gave golden petals of my Love to God, in thanks, praise and gratitude. And a golden mist I gave to Em, as I blessed him.

The next time I met with Ray, we enjoyed deep spiritual and philosophical discussions as usual, but I was mindful of my instructions to not reveal anything from Em. It was on this particular evening that Ray had said, "I am worried for your Grandmother, Cher. I hope she doesn't go into the other realm, only to realise and regret not having polished up fully, and then come to haunt you for assistance!" My Grandmother was elderly, but strong and very healthy, having been a strict vegetarian all her life. Prompts had been given to me previously that she would be passing over in the not too distant future, and this comment from Ray I took to mean that I should help her as much as she was willing to listen, regarding atoning and purifying herself before her transition. Family karma is to be taken very seriously: one must do all one can to assist one's family members, whether one wishes to or not. Em came, after I had finished my phone call with Ray, to say "It is your part to decree and give orders. Have courage, and do!"

By now, Lex had been given a good amount of time and opportunity to polish up. And, although he was honest, kind, and usually mild-mannered, he was still weak, avaricious, selfish, and unspiritual! It was clear that it wasn't just me that was feeling this way either: it was made known to me that Ray and Em felt this way too. I was prompted to pray, to see if 'we' could help to bring him up, and save his soul.

It was after this that Ray told me that he declined to meditate with any others on earth; it was now only me he would ever meditate with. We deserved each other's help, he went on to say, adding, "You are known all over the world. But don't give people too much of your essence. Let them fight for and earn your help!

Do not just give of your pearls. Few people walk the Path and live the Life because so few want to do the work! How many of your students assist you out of kindness, let alone duty? How much are they doing to assist you and others? And, how deeply are they living in tune with The Divine Plan? Help them, but don't give too much. Conserve your energy!" That night, in The Divine presence, I was told, "You are like a recruitment agency for ME. Win their souls and educate them, and bring them to ME!"

The requests coming for assistance from people in all parts of the world, including places as remote as Bhutan, was becoming overwhelming. Em said to me, "Your work has only

44

just begun. In future, you will just focus on your students, and most of the work you do to assist others can be done through the media, and your books!" He added, "Your books will be made into films. Do not let anyone possess you, for you belong to God!"

I began meditating more on deeper hidden truths, in the hope of unveiling the mystery surrounding The Great Prophet Yeshua being a member of The Team that Em, Ray, my guides and myself were a part of. I had been contemplating, and praying for a hint. Then Em came and sat with me, and said, "You have been with me since before the time of Yeshua on earth!" And, frowning, he added, "Many of those that profess to know the Great Prophet Yeshua, do not know him at all!"

As I prayed the next night, The Divine called out to me, "Light three candles, and bring ME an offering in your hands." As I did so, The Divine spoke to me again, "Some love ME in their own way. But you are MY witness. I AM with you. You Know ME. You hear ME."

I laid down on my bed to rest, and Em came, and sat casually near me. As he looked at me, there was a haze of white smoke for a few seconds, and as it disappeared, Em said, "You are expanding your consciousness in line with mine." He then said something about 'Wedding Invitations in the invisible realm', which I didn't fully understand. And then he asked if I was ready to come up higher with him? I said, "Yes" and then fell asleep. On waking, I heard The Divine voice speak to me, "The keys to Heaven, they are yours!"

The next day, after assisting my students – many of whom were doing well and having fantastic experiences and results – I sat down to rest, and an evil but sheepish-looking little entity tapped me on the shoulder as I reclined in my chair. When I turned to look at him properly, he said, "You are helping Beings out of darkness!" Before I could respond, The Divine

45

prompted me to send the Being up to the Light. As I did, his little figure was whooshed away upwards in an instant! Em came to say, "There is much work for you in America!" Then I heard the "Miaow" of my beloved boy cat, and Em said, "He will be coming back to you again!"

It was soon springtime again, and I was sitting enjoying sun-gazing when The Divine voice called out to me, "Give yourself to ME. Give ME your hand. Your hands are spotless in MY sight. Just Love ME." I couldn't stop smiling, as I was filled with ecstasy! I stayed in this state for the longest time. When I came round, I was overwhelmed by the light-headed giddiness of my Love for GOD! Em joined me later, as I lay on my bed, and said, "Swear you will stay true," and I swore that I would. He marked my third eye and told me to 'hold still' as he poured liquid white light into my heart. Then he said, "Now you will be more like me!" Before leaving, he warned me not to liberate the unworthy. I turned to him and said, "Together we can do anything!" and he turned back to look at me and replied, "Not just anything, together we can do everything!"

The next day, Em helped me with my Yoga. I had struggled with exercise due to pain, but Em had said that even though my body was delicate, I must exercise gently - and he would help me. He literally held me in the positions, and instructed me. He then reminded me that Ray's Teacher, SEG, is so fit and healthy, even in his eighties, due to team members in Spirit helping him with his Yoga. That night, I was shown my karma as a flat line – balanced – the debts paid: I am free! Em came, and said, "You should realise your station by now!" And he laughed, raising his eyebrows whilst looking at me. But I did not: not yet! Em held my face in his hands as he congratulated me and said, "Be happy, you are our representative on earth, you must be treated with reverence,

God is with you!"

I prayed to God to bless The Team, and they began to reveal more about themselves, as well as about The Divine Plan. They each showed forth their hands, and gave thanks. One of them told me to prepare, and build my Sanctuary for God. Then Em said, "The world illusion makes one think that there are limitations. There are none!" Later, alone inside The Divine presence of God, The Divine spoke these words to me, "Only the Beloved may come this close. I created you for MY work."

Ray said to me when next we spoke that he was only aware of two other people ever to have lived on earth who'd experienced the type of relationship I have with Em, adding, "I am looking forward to you becoming a Master!" Ray explained that a student may go ahead of a teacher, and reminded me that the Angel told the Prophet Muhammad that if he were to take him any further, his wings would burn, but Muhammad went ahead, and in so doing, took Gabriel up with him!

Another invitation came: this time to attend a 'White Tie' gathering of Knights and Dames, from England, Europe and Australia. One of the Knights present complimented me, "How does it feel to be so beautiful that the real you is invisible? People only see your beauty, so the real you, inside, is invisible!" I thought it to be one of the loveliest things that any stranger has ever said to me. I travelled home that night with one of the Dames, a beautiful and grand lady, and as the driver sped the car through the dark London streets, she kindly and gently asked if I should like to join their group.

It was with a heavy heart that I said goodbye to Lex. I had been told that he had goodness, and that if he didn't miss his opportunity, he would be blessed. I was also told that our connection was from Medieval times, which is why he had been given more than a fair chance. I had even visited him psychically, to tell him to bow to God, and not to money! During the few months I had spent with him, I had never once seen him offer to buy a sandwich or a bottle of water for a homeless person on the street. Nor had he ever mentioned to me any particular charity that he helped, or any philanthropic projects that he was engaged in. The last time I saw him for dinner, he chose a restaurant that had a Pig's Head as a main course option on the menu. The last time I spoke with him on the phone, it was for him to say that his father had just died!

This episode marks the last of my romantic experiments. I have not been instructed to entertain, or give any other men a chance in this way since. And many years have now passed!

CHAPTER 4
MASTERY

I wished to discuss with Em what my 'last experiment' episode had been all about. After it had been decided that communication must be broken off between me and Lex, I found myself feeling exhausted, and, just as Em had predicted, I was disappointed with Lex. Had this not been another waste of precious time? I needed clarity, so as to have peace. And I said as much. To my bemusement, Em looked at me with anger for the first time, and shouted, "Nothing is more important than God, and God's work!"

As I continued looking into Em's eyes, searching for the truth, I could tell that his feelings about this were not impartial: he was displaying powerful emotions! Suddenly, I was certain that something serious was being hidden from me. I yelled at him for an explanation. To my utter astonishment, Em yelled back at me, "I am a warrior for God, of the Highest Order. Savage murderers tried to kill me when I was on earth, but they could not, and they cannot kill you either. I won't allow it. And that man, Lex, is not worthy of you!" And, as he had said Lex's name, he spat on the floor in disgust!

Before I could quiz Em further, he vanished. I ran to the phone to call Ray. I screamed at him that I knew Em was hiding something from me, and judging by the look I had seen in Em's eyes, I was sure that his relationship with me was not just as Master and Initiate. It was something more... Ray became very grave, and serious: he told me to sit down, and slowly admitted that what I had discerned was indeed true!

In shock, I listened as Ray said that what I had unearthed was a very great secret. And that Em and I had been together since the beginning! I slammed the phone down on Ray. I felt manipulated. How could both of them have known something so serious all along and not revealed it to me? I heard Em shout, "You were not ready to know!" I began to cry as multiple scenes, images and memories flashed into my mind.

Every time Em had saved me, not just in this lifetime, but in others too. The lights in my house began flashing on and off as my rage grew. I yelled out to Em again, "All these years in isolation, all the suffering you have watched me endure, and all the times you have spoken to me of truth and trust, and you have hidden this from me. How could you?!" But Em just replied, "Even if you give up on me, do not give up on God!" Then he was silent.

In the time that it took for my rage to dissipate, I did not speak with Ray or Em at all. For the first time, I felt that I could not trust either of them. The only One I could trust was God.

I prayed and prayed to have revealed to me the meaning behind my relationship with Em. And Ray's words about me and Em having been together since the beginning: what did they mean? Over the months, in meditations, dreams and visions, and my moments of at-one-ment with The Divine, things finally started to become clear. I was told of, as well as shown details about, lives that Em and I had spent together. And, as I lay one night, struggling to understand some of the scenes I was being shown, I heard Em's voice say, "I love you, I've always loved you, since the beginning." As the scenes continued to unfold before my eyes, tears flowed as I realised how much Em had supported me throughout my incarnations. I was shown Em and I standing side by side, amongst The Team, with Yeshua at the head! It was revealed why I had endured all the horrific psychic attacks in the early years of my training: I had needed to learn to battle the evil forces as a spiritual warrior, to bring about The Divine Plan on earth through the transmutation of darkness!

I called Ray after a time, to apologise for having lost my temper: my getting angry was very rare, but it was not acceptable, and I knew that when others upset or angered me there were often terrible consequences. Ray was humble and tried to be helpful, and as our conversation ensued, he said more about our Holy Orders as a part of The Team, adding that he had not been at liberty to reveal to me the exact details of my real relationship with Em. It was a great secret that I would come to discover at some point, if and when I was ready. Then he said, "Cher, you have gone to a very high level, you will be compensated for all your suffering, and you will travel with Em and The Team, to The Divine: to Godhood! And, you will now help Em too!" I asked him what he meant by my helping Em, and he replied, "Just listen and let me finish. It is possible to even go beyond and ahead of a Master! You have a lot of power now. You don't yet know what stream Em is from. There are Beings higher than Angels and humans, you know that don't you?" I replied, "Yes, it's been revealed to me," and Ray continued, "You have passed the Initiation, Cher. We all need you!"

As I relaxed in my lounge late that evening, Em walked in. He came and sat opposite me, and smiled as he took my hands in his, calling me his 'flower of resonance' lovingly, as he asked me to forgive him. We sat with our foreheads touching gently, as he went on to say, "If Lex had treated you well, and God had approved it, I would have had to accept it. But, as he did not value highly enough the opportunity he was given, it angered me," adding that sometimes even Angels aren't good enough: God requires excellence! I said, "What do we do now?" and Em replied, "We fight for good, and carry on the work, as always." Before he left, I expressed my sorrow for having been so angry with him, and he responded by saying, "You are an Initiate, don't ever underestimate your power!" We bowed to one another before he left.

Things were now on another level between the three of us. Ray took much more of a back seat, as Em and my students quickly became my main priority. (After God, of course.) And, although I had clarity now concerning most aspects of my life, there were still the three key points that remained shrouded in mystery:

1. My companion of GOD's choosing - perhaps it was Em? 2. My position in Eternity. 3. The promise I had made to GOD.

My mystical attunement with The Divine had now increased to the point where all I felt was Love inwardly. More and more I was aware of God in me. And more and more, God spoke with me.

Em had said to me that if I wanted to know anything now, that I could ask. It might be revealed in a cryptic way at times, but from now on he would always answer what he could, and I could always ask. This stage began by Em saying, "What do you want to know?" I replied, "Anything, tell me anything that you would like for me to know regarding the work of a Master." He went on to tell me that due to the darkness created by Beings in this realm, colours and energies, as well as circumstances, often appeared to look bleak and smell rancid to The Masters. And that it was possible for a Master to feel low or sad about it, albeit temporarily, as they can transmute negativity in an instant. Em added, as he looked at me very seriously, "You must be raised up to be a Master yet! So don't let anyone talk you into anything that The Team, or God, does not approve of." I agreed, before asking him about the three key points in my life still shrouded in mystery. He answered, "The three points will be revealed in God's time, not yet!"

That night, as I tried to get off to sleep, I kept wondering what on earth I had done to end up back at the level where I had needed to come into this incarnation. Seeing that I had been with Em 'from the beginning', I must have sunk pretty low. I was aware of many instances from my past lives but had I really done so badly in all of them that I had ended up needing to come into my current incarnation? I prayed to God for wisdom.

The next night I was to experience what I can only describe as 'being in unison' with The Divine. The words sounded from 'us' in unison: "I Love YOU, MY Divine Fire." Immersed in the Bliss, I rested.

Days later, Em came to make an announcement. He said, "God is watching over you from the inside.

You don't need me anymore as a Master!" I smiled at him, as I told him that I loved him. He smiled back, and replied, "Now we are friends! Compatriots!"

After Em's statement, one of The Team told me that if I ever had to come into incarnation again, nothing would touch me!

When next I merged with The Beloved Divine, I was told to 'close down' when out in the world, so as not to attract too much attention. As I rested before sleep, Em came and said, "Our Team leads the masses Home. Nothing and no-one will be allowed to interfere with our work on The Path. Like a child being watched by its Divine Mother and Father, it will be protected!"

After saying my prayers on the next night, as I merged into The Divine Bliss, in unison the words sounded: "WE are creating the spiritual gold that the world needs."

The next day, it was imparted to me that I must move house, and quickly. I moved, with my lovely pets, to a beautiful property in London W1, on a street where both John

Lennon of The Beatles and the great Victorian writer Anthony Trollope had lived.

For a few months before relocating, I had been hearing names and tunes clairaudiently. I kept notes, sure that more would be revealed in God's time, and sure enough, in January, it was. Late one night, I 'saw' gold leaves falling all around me, and was told to stand back and observe them and let them fall into position, as they were for The Divine work. Overnight, a children's book was downloaded into my head! In the morning, The Divine instructed me to use the Holy Ash on myself. And then write out the children's book I had been 'given' during the night. The next night, during sleep, the same thing happened again. A second children's book was downloaded into my head. During the third night, several more children's stories were downloaded into my head. The Divine had prompted me to just keep writing, and so I did. I said to my sister on the phone one afternoon, "At this rate, I could end up being 'given' ten children's books," and revealed to her my experiences of being given the stories. But the next night, The Divine said, "A to Z books, to teach harmony." Within three months, The Divine had 'delivered' 26 books, along with 12 little songs for children, into my head.

One morning, I awoke with these words in my heart: "I have been arrested by Heaven, and fallen in Love with my God. And now, I have Peace and Joy."

When next The Divine spoke with me, it was to say, "It is excellent to read what the Prophets and Saints have to say about ME. But the ultimate is to hear for yourself what I, your God, have to impart to you."

Days later, I registered a message from Lex's late father, whom I had never met. (Lex had told me that his father had died when we last spoke.) The message I received was, "Please help my son, I am worried about his salvation." This type of thing happens frequently to me, but unless I am instructed to assist, or someone comes and pleads for assistance, and thus compels me to ask permission from God to intervene, then I do nothing.

I hadn't seen Ray for quite some time, but, on being prompted, I went to meet with him in one of our favourite places. We discussed The Team work, and Avatars! (Avatars are direct sparks who come from, and return to God, without any karma. All other Beings, even Masters and Angels, are making their way back to the Godhead.)

That evening, at one with The Divine, these words sounded: "Yours are the most beautiful hands, because MY power works through them. Love is the cousin of chastity."

As another spring was drawing to a close, Em came to see me, for us to take a walk together. As we strolled through the pretty London streets, we spoke of our love for God. And discussed the fact that devotion to one's Teacher or Master is in preparation for devotion to God. As we continued walking, enjoying the scenery, a man appeared in front of us, smiled at me, and said, "Yeshua loves you!" before disappearing. I turned to Em, who laughed saying, "Yeshua is calling you!" I wondered at his words as we carried on in silence for a time. Then I heard The Divine speak to me these words: "You are a spiritual warrior, ready to go into the fire for ME at any time. You are adorned with MY spiritual gold. Canonised. A Saint. A Being of Love, Fire, and MY Truth. Your hands cast forth MY Blessings, and MY Fiery Law!"

Around this time, I was approached by the media to review the Warner Bros, Hollywood movie, *Hereafter*, directed by Clint Eastwood, in which Matt Damon plays the role of a psychic. I felt that the film gave an outstandingly accurate portrayal of the beginnings of the psychic experiences of a

Medium, and those of a near-death sufferer (an experience that usually represents a much more radical shift in the individual's levels of awareness). If ever a sequel were to be made, it could be really interesting!

During a group discussion with The Team, the human Ego became the main topic. The Ego is a killer: to survive, it must lure Beings back into incarnations again and again; delving deeper and gaining more karmic debts. To live, the Ego must enjoy, indulge and express itself in the physical. During each new or successive incarnation, one must choose if the Ego will win again, or if one will do the work necessary to polish up, so that the True Spirit Self will triumph and be liberated, so as to be emancipated from the human condition. The Team presented me with a scroll at the end of the discussion. It read: "You are answerable now only to God. The narrowest path is set for you - the Beautiful Path."

Another autumn came around, and before I knew it, another winter had arrived. And I was given the news from The Divine that one of my beloved pets, my girl, was ready to go Home. I was deeply sad, but I was not tempted to do any rituals as I had not been instructed to. Instead I waited for God's timing with my girl. This period was very hard for me, but God's strength in me was not just a constant comfort, it had become a power!

One chilly afternoon, my beloved girl went Home. Only a few hours had passed when I saw her. The Divine shared with me that my girl would be 'with God' for three days, before being placed with my boy, in Em's care, until the time of their being returned to me. I was told to wait for one year, and then look to have my girl back with me on earth again, but that I would need to wait longer for my beloved boy to be returned.

A few weeks later, I went to Em's abode to sit with him,

and see my beloved boy and girl. As we sat talking, and I held my two loves in my lap, Em began to cry. I had never seen him display the emotion of sadness in this way before. He said that he had something to tell me. I sat silently, studying his face as he spoke. Tears flowed from his eyes, as he then confessed to me that he had encouraged me to come into this incarnation: that it was not purely due to my own karma! He explained as he smiled between his tears that this was one of the reasons why I used to tell my parents off when I was a child, saying, "I did not ask to be born!" (Something I remember having done often.) I was dumbfounded. He went on to say that this was also why I had so much phenomena and psychic activity around me as a child. And why the dark forces had tried to kill me off when I was small: I had endured three near-death experiences by the time I was nine years old. Tears rolled, as he went on to reveal how he had stepped in to save me from death each time. He wiped tears from his face as he apologised for how much I have suffered in this lifetime, but explained that if I came into incarnation on earth, instead of working from the invisible realms like him, much Divine work could be achieved by my sacrifice! I asked him, in as calm a state as I could, if there was anything more he was keeping from me. Plus, if it were not purely owing to my own karma that I had been brought into this incarnation, how had I built up so much negative karma to pay off? He sighed as he explained that the maya of the earth realm is a powerful illusion, and that the karma I had built up in this life was primarily due to my romantic experiments with the men in my youth. I listened intently, as he said there was more, but that it had to be revealed in God's time, when God wished for me to know. As I kissed my two loves, and got up to leave, Em bowed to me, as he called me 'Master'.

I took a three-hour walk on Hampstead Heath after I left

Em's abode: I needed to be in nature, and to be with God, without any distractions.

This concludes the period of my seven years of spiritual training.

CHAPTER 5
RAY TRAVELS ON

Almost a year had passed since I had given my beloved girl back to The Divine. And one beautiful day, in February, I was prompted to look for her on earth again. The Divine had shown me a clear vision of exactly how she looked this time around, and what markings she had to show that she was mine. Sure enough, by March I had found her. We were re-united and I brought my girl home.

The following week, as I merged with The Divine Bliss, these words were sounded: "Think about why you and Em did not incarnate together for this lifetime." I soul searched, and the revelation came. We have to be in separate realms for now, so that our dedication to God and The Divine Plan is put in first place. As Twin Flames for God, were we to incarnate together in the earth realm now, we could be distracted by the maya in this dimension, and thus distracted from our mission to lead others to spiritual emancipation.

Em came to congratulate me on having received clear information regarding our reason for being in different realms this time around. He went on to say that we are united as one in God's Will. And that I was now like him. We celebrated our love for God, and Em added, "If God asks you to marry, what will you do?" I answered that I would of course obey, if God willed it. He smiled as he proclaimed, "You are as beautiful now as you were a million years ago." When he left, I prayed for my elderly Grandmother, and two days later, my Grandmother passed on, peacefully in her sleep.

Then one morning the phone rang. It was Ray. He'd called to say that he would soon be preparing for his transition from the earthly realm, and that I was to assist him in 'getting his things in order'. He instructed me to tell no one, not even the group of spiritual aspirants he had passed on to me. This was to be a secret mission that no one on earth was to be told details of, unless and until he wished otherwise. He congratulated me on my forthcoming move, and said that I had his blessing, but that my Sanctuary for God must be built soon, for certain things had to be rooted in and sealed quickly!

Apart from taking very brief trips, I stayed In London to be close to Ray, and on hand when he needed.

We once again began to spend much of our time together in deep discussion. It was after one such evening, spent in many hours of serious dialogue with Ray, that I came home to hear another children's song, about Being Loving, downloading into my head. I had now been given 26 books, and 13 songs for children, by the Divine!

It would not be until the following January that Ray would allow me to reveal his 'plans' to any of Our Team here on earth. Aspirants at a certain point are very much considered as family members, as well as a part of The Team – should they complete their training periods! Many of them were deeply concerned that Ray had been out of reach for the best part of a year, and many of them had been calling me to see if I would tell them any news of him. But of course I did not. I would always hint that Ray was very busy, which was true. During those last months, we wrote much and spoke much, and put his house in order, so to speak. One of his most pressing concerns was that he didn't wish to leave his tail behind him in this dimension at all: all his loose ends were to be tied up, all plans to be made, and any and all of his last wishes to be perfectly set in place and carried out.

During Ray's preparatory period he was visited by his Teacher, SEG. This made him immensely happy. SEG is much older than Ray, and to this day he is still going strong, continuing on the work. It was around this time, when Ray and I had been discussing the powers and forces in this dimension, that Em came to pray together with us in The Divine presence and we all heard the message that Ray would go to God.

The chilly dark nights soon turned to milder evenings, as I made my way to and from Kensington to see Ray. Then one day he said that he was ready for me to notify one or two of the aspirants, so they might come to see him before he travelled on. The two people in question came immediately. As we sat with him, he spoke with his usual joyful lilt as he encouraged his two aspirants. Then, on turning to me, his voice became very serious, and as he stared in my direction he uttered, "You can carry on the work as a Master!"

A few nights later, I heard Em calling out to Ray. Then psychically, as I lay in my bed, I saw Ray being carried by his arms as Em and another member of The Team came to assist him as he prepared to loose his body. Afterwards, Ray appeared to be shining! Then I heard Em say to Ray, "It's all right, Cher is on earth to carry on the work!" Ray turned to look at me and smiled as he raised his hand to wave. I waved and smiled back at him, as we thanked each other for all the assistance. Tears welled in my eyes, and Ray called out, "Don't worry, we have Eternity, Cher!" Ray then withdrew with Em and the other Being to discuss matters, and I fell into a deep but brief sleep. On waking, The Divine spoke these words to me: "Step up and take your place as a World Teacher," while a symbol of white light shone out through my forehead.

Within a few hours, Ray had travelled on. Before leaving this earthly realm, he'd said to me, "Love is the highest power. Not love born of passion. But Divine Love." As he made his transition, I saw Ray with Em, preparing for his next stage of the eternal journey. Ray turned to me and said, "I am free, and will never be in chains again, and neither will you. God has blessed us. Be happy." The following night, Ray appeared to me to give me a message: "Make it your life's work to do more good than I did!"

CHAPTER 6
MYSTERY SCHOOLS

I was called by Em to attend a meeting in one of the lecture halls at The Invisible University. This was to be the first time that I would come to see such a vast number of The Team assembled together in one place.

Before disclosing anything further, I am permitted to share some information regarding Mystery Schools. Although it is believed, and often written, that these Esoteric Schools of Higher Learning are located in the physical realm, that is not true: the schools are mystical! There are certain sacred spaces and sites on earth that the energy of Mystery Schools may be found, but they are not in physical buildings. I am also pressed to reveal that these hidden schools are run by Spiritual Beings or 'Intelligences' that are not in physical earthly bodies. These Beings may be Masters who have incarnated on earth previously; they may also be Great Teachers and Prophets who have left the earthly realm. And they may also at times be Beings that have never taken on physical incarnations! As previously mentioned, there are streams of Beings that are higher than Angels and humans.

Initiates may be invited to attend, if and when they are ready, to study at any of these hidden schools.

Here, they will be afforded the opportunity to learn about Elemental Forces, Devas, Mineral Powers, Symbols, Rituals, Metaphysics, Akasha, Adepthood, Universal Law, Spiritual Law, Realms of Existence, Mysticism, Mastery, Christhood, Godhood, and Divine Will.

I wish to share also, that just because a person may be interested in esotericism, and may even go so far as to seek out a Teacher, unless and until the person has transmuted the darkness within themselves, and cleared the channels between their lower and higher self, no access to a Mystery School can be permitted. For it is not even the decision of a Teacher to admit an aspirant into the Inner Realms of Higher Learning: it is only the energy from the unique vibration resonated from within the purified Soul, which alerts the Masters and Spiritual Beings in the hidden realms that another aspirant is now ready to respond to the Divine call.

The Mystery Schools stand as gateways to knowledge of The Divine Plan. Through the Spiritual Laws of Love and Harmony, twinned with selflessness, an aspirant admitted to these hidden schools comes to study the secrets of Wisdom and Truth. These secrets are not for those still assailed by the lower mind, rooted in selfishness. For knowledge becomes power, and power in the wrong hands leads to further darkness.

Barriers of all kinds must be torn asunder: not just barriers of race and creed, but of species and beings! Unity must be realised. Fear must be vanquished. Darkness must become Light. Wrongs must be righted.

Ray had revealed to me long ago that 'We Beings' have created death and the devil! With our own thoughts, words, and deeds. The teachings of all Mystery Schools are clear that herein lies the curse of humankind. For the debts of karma owed are not just between humankind alone. The debts owed to our brethren, our little brothers and sisters of the Animal Kingdom, are mighty indeed. Man breaks the Law of Harmony and the Law Divine by killing and destroying God's Creation, be it by greed of palate, wanton fun or sport, and by every act of suffering humankind causes, it seals its own fate, making it impossible for Peace to reign on earth. Until every debt is repaid, to all Beings, humankind must suffer in the lower realms of existence. It is Divine Law!

The Divine Plan must be made manifest, for it is the will of God. And the Great Guardians of Evolution will continue to work to that end. On that note, I will now return to the meeting in the lecture hall at The Invisible University.

As we entered the large lecture hall, I had expected Em to stay with me and take a seat, but to my surprise he stepped up to the dais to make an announcement, and with his eyes motioned for me to step forward. As I did so, the large number of The Team members watched in silence. Em stood me by his side as he shared with the crowd that I had been called as a World Teacher, and that they were all to support me in the work.

As we stepped down from the dais, Em suggested that we stay on, and listen to the lecture that would begin shortly. It was to be on Karma, Destiny and Free Will.

CHAPTER 7
KARMA, DESTINY, AND FREE WILL

Em and I sat beside one another as we listened to the lecture. Much was taught about The Mystic Way, esoteric and exoteric practices, and the fruits that are born therefrom.

The lecturer continued, saying that Incarnated Beings are all 'tourists' in the physical dimension. Once aware of this reality, one is so humbled that selfish abuse of others, be they human, animal or the earth itself, becomes impossible. We are all responsible for our own 'roles' in 'life'. Do you feel ready to meet your God and stand boldly as the Holy co-creator that The Divine willed for you to be? If not, then there is work for you to do on you! Build a relationship with The Divine. It is the only one that exists eternally in reality!

Much was spoken of in relation to living harmlessly, and how it is one of the fastest and most effective ways to build light and transmute darkness. The audience listened attentively as they were instructed to feed the body spiritual (harmless) foods, feed the mind with meditation and spiritual literature, and feed the Spirit with prayer and silence!

The talk then turned to the interconnected aspects between Karma, Destiny, and Free Will...

Karma - Karma is the law of cause and effect. It is what keeps a Being trapped in the cycle of suffering and reincarnation: a slave to your own lower self, until the point of transmutation of your own shadow. You are you forever – thus what you create, you are responsible for. As co-creators with The Divine, every thought, word and action will create 'something' that is either light or dark, and, over time, those thoughts, words, and deeds crystallise, both within you, and in the world around you. Sometimes, the light or the dark you have been bringing into existence will crystallise into forces, and even into Beings! To be above karma, through self-purification, and living without causing harm to others, or to the self, is the road to emancipation. Liberation!

Destiny - Does one need to be a slave to destiny? Yes, it is a law, unless and until one can transcend one's destiny. In the grand scheme of things, The Divine has allotted a certain destiny for each Being, as a part of The Divine Plan. That destiny being supremely good, and in alignment with Divine Will. But due to each Being having brought karmic debts upon itself during its devolution, it is subject to the ramifications and repercussions of its negative fate and destiny, until the balance of karmic debts is repaid. The Being can then choose, if you will, to transcend its destiny, so long as its choices are harmless!

Free will - The Divine has bestowed the power of free will upon all Beings. One may choose to be good or evil, and thus either create more karmic debt, or transmute existing karmic debt. Likewise, you are either building more light within oneself and the world around you, or adding to the darkness within and around you. How do we define what is good or evil? By whether it causes harm or harmony! And, whether or not it is in alignment with Divine Law and Divine Will. The Divine Will is for all Beings to be in harmony. Once a Being is living in harmony with itself and others, it may choose to use its free will without karmic repercussions!

Thus we see, ultimately, that karma, destiny, and free will are interconnected. As the lecture came to a close, Em turned to me to say, "Yeshua has called you!"

CHAPTER 8

YESHUA

I was escorted to the entrance of a beautiful and grand building, and told to climb the stone steps to the edifice before me, alone. As I walked up the steps, I began to feel supremely happy and blissful. When I reached the top, these words were called out to me from a large open doorway, "Cher of God, come inside."

When I stepped inside, Yeshua appeared! The light that was radiating from The Great Prophet illumined everything in sight, including me. Yeshua smiled as he walked me to a magnificent room. I have since come to call this room The Holy Office. Yeshua motioned with his hands for me to sit on one of the majestic chairs. Feelings of awe welled within me as he stood regally before me.

"You have become Holy again," Yeshua said, as he held my gaze. "Thanks to God, I have, yes," I replied. Yeshua smiled at my response, saying, "We must all thank God for everything. For even The Prophets and The Masters are but examples: GOD is the goal!" Yeshua turned his face for a moment, before turning back to fix his eyes on mine, saying, "You have questions, so ask them." I paused before uttering, "My Teacher Ray told me that you did not die: is that true?" Yeshua answered with power in his voice, "I ascended, I cannot die, for I am eternal." He then asked if I remembered the time that I was a Carmelite Monk. The scenes of that lifetime flashed into my memory, and I had no choice but to reply, "Yes!" at which he smiled.

Next, I asked Yeshua about the religions of earth. He replied by saying, "God has no religion. Religions are frameworks to help people to realise God." His eyes flashed as he added, "Many of The Prophets and Great Masters and Teachers transcended the religious frameworks they were born into. God requires that Beings be kind, peaceful, loving, joyful and harmless, to glorify their Divine Creator!"

I asked The Great Prophet about The Bible. He replied, "Which Bible?", with a smile. I smiled back as I said, "The Holy Bible." He nodded to show that he knew all along what I meant. I was acutely aware that Yeshua knew everything I was going to ask him well in advance. His reply was enlightening: "The Holy Bible was written over a period of more than 1500 years, by more than forty authors. Many of the original texts were omitted from inclusion, as Constantine attempted to keep the peace. Some of the original texts, The Gnostic Gospels, have been found and revealed to the world. Other texts are yet to be put before the public, and still others are yet to be discovered for the Beings on earth to marvel at!"

I asked about Mary of Magdala, more modernly known as Mary Magdalene. Yeshua resounded, "It is blasphemous for people to accuse Mary of being a prostitute. It is true that seven demons were cast out of her, namely Darkness, Desire, Ignorance, Fear, Pedantry, Foolish Reason, and Self-Righteousness. All aspects of the lower self. Since the time of Pope Gregory in the sixth century, the life of Mary of Magdala has been misconstrued. Mary, whilst on earth, became an Initiate and one of my chief Apostles, along with John."

I was about to ask another question when Yeshua interjected: "I first came to you in a vision in your current lifetime when you were 19 years old: do you remember?" I felt uneasy, and apologised to him for having taken so long in this incarnation to polish up. He looked at me seriously as he said, "I have watched your progress since your return to earth, to wait for you to realise your position!" He paused before adding, "You may ask one more question now. And then come to my 'Holy Office' on other occasions, for further discussions." I thanked him and proceeded to ask, somewhat nervously, about The Divine Plan for earth. He replied, "Much is known to you already. But I will add this for now: God requires the sacrifice of human egos, the transmutation of the shadow. Animals that are sacrificed are pleasing only to the evil lower forces! Which is why when on earth, I lost my temper with the men who were selling doves to be sacrificed. And, why there was only bread and wine at my Last Supper. One of God's Divine Laws is to not kill!"

As I was leaving The Holy Office, I turned to Yeshua and said, "How did you find the strength to go through with the crucifixion?" and he answered, "I focused on God, and God's Will alone." When I said to him, "You must be The Greatest Being ever to have been on the earth!" he smiled, and said, "Almost!"

CHAPTER 9
THE DIVINE PLAN

God's Divine Plan was set before the Creation of the Worlds and time were made manifest. The Divine Plan of The Creator encompasses all of Creation being holy, joyful, peaceful, creative and in perfect harmony.

Many consider that Creation is for the purpose of humankind alone. It is not. It is for all things manifest to glorify God. The role humankind has to play in this earthly dimension is one of steward and caretaker. Spiritual power comes with responsibility. The more realised a Being is, the more they will be compelled to assist their fellow Beings, and all of Creation. Not just as a matter of duty, but as of an uprising of compassion from the indwelling Spirit of The Divine. God's instructions to humankind – Be stewards of the earth and take care of all other Beings – meaning not to kill, or to eat other Beings as if they are fruits, for the foods God has created for humans are manifested from the ground, be they herbs, vegetables, grains or fruits.

As the earthly world begins to align itself with The Divine Plan set for it before the beginning of time and Creation, it can expect the emergence of a peaceful, heavenly plane of existence, governed by love and compassion. For the redemption of Beings is in tune with Divine purpose. The law of Karma, God's Fiery Law, is for correction, not punishment.

The Prophets and Masters assert that there is indeed such a thing as a human community, and that the aspirant enhances their spirituality by according credence to this principle. But The Prophets and Masters will add that all sentient Beings, including those who are in Spirit, are bonded together in so far as they are all engaged on an evolutionary march as part of the creative process of The Divine. And that not only an action but a mere thought from a sentient creature has an impact on cosmic life embracing all of evolving Beings, including humans, Mighty Intelligences and Angelic Hosts, as well as the animal and elemental kingdoms!

While it is true that the unfolding process carries religious implications, it is esoteric and not necessarily scriptural and dogmatic. Working one's path into the ethereal realms is an inner experiential search for Divine Truth, underlain by an unfolding evolutionary process. The Prophets and Masters do not object to institutionalised scriptural and confessional religion, but they proffer time-worn advice to fellow seekers about the danger of the Transcendent being fossilised when set within a rigid framework. The Prophets and Masters have warned of the search for Spiritual Illumination being stifled by exoteric traditions and practices alone. To achieve attunement with God, one must know God experientially. God consciousness involves understanding that all Beings, both male and female, are equal in essence – in perfect balance – as manifestations of God. In the unmanifest, pre-existent state, male and female are One. This Truth holds within it the gnosis, which unveils the mystery of Love and becoming One with God again.

I conclude *The Hidden Truths* revealed in this manuscript of the second *Modern Seer* book in the year 2011.

Self Help and Improvement

Introduction

As a Spiritual Adviser, I suggest to clients and my students alike that being spiritual involves living a good life, which requires practical application. It is not enough to merely read about, think about, or even discuss living a good and spiritual life: one must apply techniques to ensure positive transformational results!

The following techniques, if applied with pure motives, could change one's life simply yet dramatically, for the betterment of all. Be always mindful that you as a Being have power, and that everything that you think, do and say will either add to the light within you and thus in the world around you, or add to the darkness within you and thus in the world around you.

I wish you well on your evolutionary journey! May The Divine guide you.

Thought Control Deal

Choosing to have good thoughts is a powerful step. I emphasise the word choosing, for the simple reason that your thoughts are your own: you should be able (with some effort) to choose which type of thoughts you allow in your mind. Be in charge! If you do not like the thought patterns that have crystallised in your mind over time; if they are not good and positive, choose not to allow them any more.

Here is a technique: as a negative thought arises within your thought field, stop it immediately. Don't allow it to run into a chain of thoughts, stop it at the first negative thought. And, if necessary, say to yourself inwardly, or aloud if you wish, "I choose to have good, positive, productive, happy thoughts." Just as you would not allow rubbish to keep flying into your home, do not allow negative thinking to invade your inner home!

SPEECH RULES DEAL

It is written in the spiritual laws of speech that if what you have to say is not true, necessary and kind, you should not say it! Words have power. And just as thoughts crystallise and manifest over time, so do words – except that the impact of words in the earthly realm is instant. Be sure that your words do not humiliate others. If you have a grievance to address with someone, speak truthfully, calmly, and say only what is necessary. Make your words edifying, not derogatory. Ultimately, speak only if your words will have more of a positive or correctional impact than your silence!

HARMLESS ACTIONS DEAL

As you learn to empower yourself with the Thought Control and Speech Rules techniques above, you should find it much easier, and indeed more natural, for your actions to become harmless. Violence is the lowest form of communication, meaning that one has so little Mastery over oneself and one's emotions, that one has to resort to the lowest negative impulse – an act of violence. If you feel rage rising from within, do not act on it, just watch and observe it. If possible, step into the fresh air, put on some music, or even better watch or look at something funny! Within moments, rage dissipates if it is not acted upon. The more you practice this technique, the more peace you will have, and will invite into your life.

SOCIALISING DEAL

Who you choose to have in your personal space is important. Your home should be your sanctuary and place of peace and happiness. Choose carefully whom you invite into your personal space. All Beings emit vibrations: if you do not feel good vibes from someone, do not have them in your space. That is not to say you can't help people who may be in trouble or experiencing difficulties. But if you can help them by an uplifting phone call or by making a positive suggestion, do so, instead of having them in your home.

KINDNESS DEAL

Kindness is a strength, not a weakness! Being kind means that you are thinking, speaking, acting and living for the betterment of all Beings. Not just humans, and not just yourself. Discipline is a close cousin of kindness. If you are not being disciplined with yourself, or your loved ones, you are not really being kind. Positive, good and structured discipline is a prerequisite for living a good life. If you mistake kindness for weakness and overindulge yourself or your loved ones, emotionally or otherwise, you won't be contributing to the evolutionary process. And thus not benefitting the Being in question. Be kind!

DATING DEAL

If you should find yourself in the experimental phase of dating, be safe and savvy! For instance, when speaking with someone new for the first time, don't reveal too much, keep things on a need-to-know basis. And if you get to the stage where you agree to meet for a date, go in the daytime, and meet just for coffee at a café, not at your home, or theirs! This will mean that the maximum of an hour need be all the time you spend, and it won't cost much money either. Many people spend long hours wasting not only their time, but also that of the person they've met for a date. Not to mention the vast amounts of money spent at restaurants, or, even worse, on alcohol during a dinner that neither party really wishes to be at! If you find that after a few coffee dates you wish to go for dinner, you will both be more sure of each other by then, and will have had the chance to get to know one another a bit. Keep your address confidential until you are very sure of the person you are dating!

SEX ENERGY DEAL

There is an exchange of psychic energy that takes place between sexual partners. This is not to do with the obvious physical exchange of fluids, but with psychic energy! This is one of the reasons why people may be platonic friends for years and be attracted to and even flirt with one another and still be okay emotionally, so long as they have not had sex with each other. The moment that the sex energy is exchanged, one or other feels that they are emotionally connected, perhaps deeply so, and may even feel that something is now owed to them by the other person, be it a relationship or marriage! Play safe, emotionally, physically and psychically!

MARRIAGE DEAL

If you should find yourself on the 'family path' and in a marriage or about to get married, be ready for responsibility on all fronts! When couples marry, it is not just the karma of one another that they are volunteering, or, more accurately, vowing to carry; it is also the karma of both extended families. Karma is now about the group. It is both noble and brave to get married or more accurately, send a signal to the cosmos and God that you are willing and ready to carry and assist another Being and their family, as well as your own. Be very sure before you make this step, as, once the commitment is made, it is very difficult to break karmically! It may be relatively easy to divorce legally, but emotionally and karmically the bonds once made are very strong!

FAMILY DEAL

Family members, be they children, siblings, parents or spouses, are all karmically connected. It is part of one's duty, in line with living a good life, to look to the needs of, and assist, one's family members. If you have reached a stage, which many do, where there are breaks in the family links, and communication is difficult, you may for a certain time prefer to keep physical contact to a minimum. But you must still support – psychically and financially – one's dependents. If you have children, you have co-created them and brought them into this world, and you are responsible for them!

CREATIVITY DEAL

Go deep into your interior and discover what moves you.

Each Being is unique, and bestowed with gifts by The Divine Creator. Find out what your gifts are by searching within your heart and mind. What bothers you most in this world? What makes you most happy? What would you change about the world if you could?

Meditate on the three things. And when the energy emerges to spur you on, aim with all your might to fulfil your destiny! You may invent the next top tech gadget. You may discover the next breakthrough in Science. You may even save the planet from environmental disaster! There are no limits!

KARMA DEAL

Balancing one's karma is one of the main reasons for being on earth! So before you leave this dimension, be sure that you have done everything to clear your karmic debt. If you owe someone something, settle it, be it money or an apology. Tie up loose ends. Don't leave your tail behind you. Be practical. Anyone can be taken from this earth at any time: it is not just the elderly and the unwell who should live this way. The most spiritual way to live is to be happy and free karmically, so you are ready to meet your Divine Creator in any given moment. Be it via Mystical attunement, or by dying and leaving this world!

DIET DEAL

Eat foods that you like and that suit your body, so long as they are harmless! Meaning that no other Being has had to suffer or be tortured or murdered for you to eat! Regulate the times you eat. Your body is a machine, or more accurately a creature. So eat at certain times each day. If you can, have only two meals a day. In between your two meals, eat fruit or nuts and seeds if they suit. Have treats, but sparingly, and not every day. If you eat this way, your body will function at optimum levels, and you will not need to crash diet.

EXERCISE DEAL

Walking, yoga and swimming are some of the best forms of exercise for the human creature. As a machine, your body needs exercise to keep everything running smoothly. Whether you choose to exercise alone at home, out in nature, or in a gym, get moving and enjoy. Exercise is good for the mind and body, and if done correctly, it can lift the Spirit too!

GIVING DEAL

As part of living a good life, giving is paramount. It need not always be money you give; it may be your time or your advice. Try and be mindful of opportunities to give. Be helpful. Small things can count in big ways. Remember that every breath you take is a gift given to you; it is not yours. If it were yours, you wouldn't need to rely on the air to breathe! I encourage my students to give to others, especially to the needy and vulnerable, in a variety of ways. Give, and see how happy it makes you!

FAITH DEAL

Having Faith is key to living a good and spiritual life. Faith in oneself and Faith in The Divine... All Beings on earth are subject to the vicissitudes of life in this realm, beset with tests and trials. It is said by The Masters that either the world can teach you, or God can teach you. If God teaches you, empowerment will follow! Have Faith in the steps you are taking in your aim to live a good life. Have Faith in your children and your loved ones. Build Faith from within until it crystallises from your Spirit in to your thought life! It is written that without Faith, it is impossible to please God.

MEDITATION DEAL

Meditate and go within to find your place of peace inside of your heart. Meditation is the key, the ticket, if you will, to overcoming the lower self. You must seek, peacefully. Train the mind to be silent at your command. Immerse yourself in the inner bliss that resides in your higher self, as the powerful, loving you. If you prefer to meditate to music or in silence, or even chanting, do so with the intention of finding God within you.

FORGIVENESS LIST 1

Write a very detailed list of every one and everything you need to forgive. Include all people, writing down their names or initials on the list so as to psychically release any negative links you're harbouring towards them. Include all events or instances that you need to forgive, and any and every thought, word, or act that needs to be forgiven. This may well be an ongoing list if one is to be thorough. In carrying out this exercise, should any prompts come for you to stretch out to any of the people on the list to apologise to them, for example, or even perhaps send a gift as a peace offering, expecting nothing in return, then make your apology gently and with humility. If you still feel anger towards anyone, pray for the strength to forgive them.

FORGIVENESS LIST 2

Write a very detailed list of every single thing that you need to ask God to forgive you for. Include every thought, word, and act that you need to. This will be an ongoing exercise. My Teacher Ray, continued this practice every day of his life until he travelled on, and he was a holy man! It is a powerful exercise, and helps tremendously in building a relationship with The Divine. For it is written that if you do not forgive, you cannot go to God.

HAPPINESS LIST

Make a list of all the things that make you happy. Not the obvious things like shopping, or cars. Go deep into your Being and discover the things that make you truly happy. If you like nature, be in it often and study it. Find out what about it makes you most happy. Smile often, until it becomes natural. Make a commitment to yourself to laugh everyday. Watch and listen to funny things. Value humour. Laughter is God's music!

POWER PRAYER

God is all-powerful! Be humble and respectful when you pray, in the knowledge that God is mighty and able to do anything! Be sure to have worked on your two Forgiveness Lists before engaging in prayer. Then, clearly, without repetition – for God hears you before you even ask – pray to The Divine for assistance.

SILENT PRAYER

Praying in silence could ideally be carried out after the Power Prayer. Clear your mind of all thoughts. Ask for nothing. Be still physically, and silent mentally. And sit and wait. When The Divine presence envelops you, God may speak to your heart or mind in the silence. Be thankful and grateful at the close of prayer.

SPIRITUAL TRAINING

The Spiritual Path is beset with test, trials and many contradictions. (See the first book *The Hidden Secrets of a Modern Seer.*) And an aspirant is expected to become highly practical as well as responsible during the testing times. Asceticism is an important part of training, along with carrying on one's duties in the world.

Many of my students in the early days wondered if they should run off to the Himalayas or leave their families and go into isolation for their training. God expects you to train wherever you are! I have a friend who is a Monk, who was trained in isolation as it was his destiny, and who had no family or dependents when he was instructed to live on the celibate hermetic life path. Yet when he had completed his years of training, he was sent to live in New York City! The Path is not for the faint-hearted, and most Teachers are very strict. Indeed, I have been told several times that I can be harsh as well as strict. But honouring your responsibilities, as well as honouring your body and your word, is a part of honouring your Spirit and God.

PSYCHIC ATTACKS

Psychic attacks are paranormal events usually triggered by negative flows of energy in the unseen realms. Under their influence, a person experiences an overwhelming onrush of unpleasant emotions and irrational fears. Victims at times have had entities in the shape of half-formed humans and creatures manifest before them, invading their auric field – or even poltergeists! These attacks can happen to ordinary men and women, as well as to children and to all grades of spiritual aspirants, including advanced mystics.

Psychic attacks usually stem from two sources. They may originate as telepathic negative flows from the psychic world of one's fellow humans, who are either using rituals, magic and wilful thoughts, or who unwittingly send harmful vibrations (unwittingly, because malicious gossip and bad thoughts about people can infect their psychic space with debilitating and harmful energy). They could also derive from discarnate beings in the form of ghosts and poltergeists roaming the invisible realms. These entities could show up in the waking state and in dreams, possibly even physically attacking you or moving objects around in the home. They may project a menacing and frightening energy as well as emitting an unpleasant smell. They can tell you lies, whisper, shout and terrify you or even engage in a visible act of violence, as a human would. It is possible for them to be seen either as shadows or in full manifestation!

The following are techniques which one could apply in coping with or handling psychic attacks. (See also my first book *The Hidden Secrets of a Modern Seer.*)

Number 1

Protection Technique: Close your eyes and visualize a powerful white light enveloping and protecting your entire being. Do not use a mirror effect as a shield around your light of protection, as the energies will be mirrored back to you if the dark forces are coming from within you! Ask The Divine to keep you safe.

Number 2

Meditate and Pray: This will help you to achieve the spiritual strength needed to fight your psychic battles. Create a sacred place in which to meditate and pray regularly. It is also possible to meet and interact with your Spirit Guides and Divine Helpers using inner focusing techniques.

Number 3

Spiritual Cleansing Ritual: Sage is just one of the ideal herbs to be dried and burned. Light it as you would incense, and pray that you and your place be cleansed psychically, allowing the smoke to billow around yourself and into the rooms of your home. Keep the ashes in the soil of a plant you have in your home.

Number 4

Mantra: Focusing on and remembering The Divine is imperative. Use the name that represents your Creator. Repeat the words 'I Love God', The Divine, Allah, Krishna, Buddha, Almighty, Yahweh or Elohim, again and again in your mind. Speak it out loud, or shout it out if necessary when under a psychic attack!

Number 5

Spiritual Practitioner: An experienced spiritual practitioner can help you – depending on how open you are to guidance – to search for the relevant ritual and healing techniques needed. The practitioner may even have knowledge of holy and secret remedies and mixes from the plant and mineral kingdoms. It is likely that you will be advised to avoid alcohol and drugs, as well as to read certain spiritual books, and keep good company.

ANGELIC HELPERS

Angels are powerful Beings, and like humans, can be both good and evil as they are still evolving back up to the Godhead. They are androgynous (neither completely male or female, but a combination of both) and multidimensional (meaning that they can function in and impact upon both the physical and invisible realms of existence). Good Angels serve God and can assist other Beings, including humans, that are servants of God. If you are ever in tune with a Being from another realm, be sure to always test it. A good Being will never instruct you to do bad things, to yourself or any other Beings, including animals. A good Being will always be harmless, helpful and supportive. If you have a good Angel, you are blessed!

FOR GOD

This is the most important section of this chapter! Most people, even spiritual people, rarely think about what they can do for God. Mostly it is the case that humans want something from God, even if it is forgiveness.

Lots of spiritual aspirants will say that they love God, but what do they do to show that they love God? When did you last do something for God? Think deeply about this. I wish to be clear that by praying and meditating, you are not doing something for God. And it is not that God requires for you to do anything but love your Divine Creator. But when you do things for God, selflessly, out of pure love, miracles may happen!

CASE STUDIES

INTRODUCTION

The majority of my time is now spent in training my students, and writing, as I have mentioned earlier. Examples that I am revealing here are but a few, to show the ways in which the streams of power can flow through me. Not from me, by choice, but through me, by Divine decree. I explained in Chapter 2 that after my experience on the night that the lightning touched my hands, things became much more intense. The powers that flow and manifest are as a part of God's Higher Spiritual Law. It is neither my decision nor my doing, but what happens to people when they meet me or speak with me, is to do with their karma being quickened and played out, and, if you will, blessed or judged by the powers that be.

I reiterate that The Divine revealed to me that as a worker for The Divine Plan, it is a part of my duty to have certain blessings, commands and judgments flow through me. Not from me, but through me. What I reveal regarding examples of events, may seem shocking to you the reader, but I assure you, when these instances take place, they are just as shocking to me. I hasten to add that on occasions, I have got on my knees to plead and pray to God that no harm may come to someone who has angered or annoyed me or spoken blasphemously in my presence, as it's often the case that people who do so, suffer tragic consequences. Conversely, many miraculous blessings have manifested through me for people, regardless of whether or not I may feel that they are worthy or deserving. It is God's Will, not mine.

Needless to say, confidentiality is a top priority in my work and for this very reason I will not be disclosing the names and identities of my private clientele.

DOUBLE BLESSING

The daughter of a British Nobleman had asked to see me for assistance. It was sanctioned, and so I agreed to meet with her. The lady in question was happily married but in all the years she and her husband had been together, they had not been able to conceive a child. I was prompted to instruct the lady to avoid meat and alcohol, as well as to pray and adhere to spiritual principles, in preparation for our meeting. On the day in question, The Divine guided me to pray with the lady, as well as to place my hands on her abdomen. The lady thanked me, and I left. Very shortly after our meeting, she conceived, and soon bore two children.

MARITAL BLESSING

A very shy and fearful woman was put in touch with me by one of my clients. The woman had been suffering domestic abuse by her husband for many years. She wept as she relayed some of the horrific experiences her husband had subjected her to. Everything from sexual abuse to violence, as well as threats to take her life! I did my best to remain impartial, as relationships are karmic. But the woman pleaded for my help. A few days had passed when The Divine urged me to prepare some sacred items to send to the woman: I did not need to meet her in person, or go to her home, I was just guided to send them to her, which I did.

Her husband has not abused or assaulted her from that day to this. He has no idea of the conversation I had with his wife, nor of what power The Divine infused within the sacred items as I prepared them, to assist them in their marriage.

FAMILY BLESSING

The Divine had revealed to me that the father of a student of mine would be making his transition and passing over suddenly. I was instructed to enlighten my student and to say that things had been revealed as a blessing so that any underlying issues in their relationship could be addressed and healed, to balance the karma before the father's passing, and for them to enjoy the short time he had left on earth as a family. I was also advised to instruct my student to encourage their parents to sell their large property and buy a smaller home in preparation, so that the mother would not have to cope with the stress of doing such things alone, once the father had passed on. All of which they did. And shortly afterwards, whilst out on a lovely walk in nature, the father of my student died suddenly and peacefully.

SON BLESSING

A young couple had been told by specialists that they couldn't have any more children. But the young lady had been shown in dreams that she was going to have a son! So convinced was she of the fact that she was meant to have a son, she said she was going to sell the family home to pay for fertility treatments until it manifested. They had been trying for six years but she still hadn't fallen pregnant. On this occasion, God revealed to me that the young lady was correct to believe her dreams: she was destined to have a son. So, as The Divine had instructed me, I suggested that the young lady have a little holy statue on display in the family home, and well as undertaking good deeds and acts of kindness to accompany certain prayer techniques. Three months later she was pregnant. And their son was born at Christmas!

DAUGHTER BLESSING

A mature lady reached out to me for assistance after having gone through very painful and traumatic times having unsuccessful IVF treatments. She didn't have any supportive family around her, and due to loneliness in her marriage she was suffering greatly by the time I had been instructed to help her. It was revealed to me that she had terminated a baby when she was only in her teenage years, and since then had not been able to get pregnant! She cried and expressed deep remorse as I explained to her that The Divine was waiting for her to atone before she could be blessed with a child. The lady was by now almost fifty years old! I was prompted to teach her specific prayer techniques as well as instruct her to live spiritually, and to atone.

Within months, her marriage was strengthened and she became pregnant. And The Divine gave her the blessing of giving birth to her beautiful baby daughter!

LIFE SAVING BLESSING

One of my students had told me that they had planned to take a trip to a certain country just days before they were due to fly. As we sat discussing the trip, The Divine gave me a prompt that it was not necessary for the trip to go ahead, and that my student ideally should stay in England for now, and take the trip to that country at another time. I relayed this to my student, who didn't seem too pleased, and asked if they should just cancel the trip, even though all the arrangements had now been made. I replied, "It is up to you to decide, you have free will." And it was left at that. My student took the trip, and after a week or so passed, my student rang in distress. The plane on the return flight home had been given the okay by Air Traffic Control and had taken off, but had to do an emergency crash landing due to another plane being in the same flight path directly ahead! As the plane came down and slid across the runway, my student prayed to God for a blessing for all Beings on the plane to survive the crash landing unscathed. The blessing was granted. I reprimanded my student as they arrived at my home in tears. They had been warned in advance that the trip was not necessary!

PROJECT BLESSING

The idea for a big international project had been the passionate focus of a client of mine for many years. But, it was only when my client began living a good and spiritual life, and then vowed that the project, were it to manifest, would be used as a platform to assist with The Divine Plan, that The Divine granted a blessing for the project. Literally everyone and everything needed to bring the project into existence, including vast sums of money, miraculously manifested! And the project was birthed.

PRICELESS POSSESSIONS BLESSING

I took my car to a garage to be serviced, and on speaking with the mechanic was shown a horrible flash vision. As the mechanic continued taking details as well as my car keys, The Divine told me that the man's last remaining possessions on earth were going to go up in flames! I did my best to retain composure as I 'watched' and listened inwardly to what had been revealed. I was then advised to relay the information to the mechanic, who looked at me in horror. He said that his sports car, along with his late mother's jewellery, which was in the glove compartment of his car, was all that he had left in the world. His parents had died suddenly and left him a large inheritance, which he had spent recklessly due to his grief. I urged him to remove the items of his late mother's that he had in the glove box, as if he left them in there they would not be salvaged. Needless to say, the mechanic was very shaken by my prediction, but he did as suggested. A week later, he called to tell me that his car had been torched by vandals, but that thanks to my warning, he still had his most priceless possessions: his late mother's jewellery!

WORST NIGHTMARE

It had been revealed to me that the man here mentioned was arrogant, boastful and full of false pride. He had strung many women along over the years, never committing to any of them, yet was happy to have sex with them all on a casual basis. The man had managed to live most of his adult life in this way. That is until he was introduced to me. As he sat and talked openly, as many people find themselves doing, often involuntarily, when in my company, he blurted out that his worst nightmare would be for him to get caught: for one of the women he was having sex with to trick him and get themselves pregnant, and then rob him of his fortune! Then he laughed it off as he said to me that he thought it could never happen, not to him, after all it had never happened as yet! Weeks after he had said it to me, it happened!

WRONGLY ACCUSED

A lively discussion, which had led to a heated debate, caused a female contributor to lose her temper. As I stood and watched her silently, her temper began to rise, to the point where she was shouting at those assembled, before turning to both accuse and insult me. She then stormed out. The female in question had lost her temper unnecessarily and had falsely accused and insulted me. On storming out of the building, she was struck down in the road by a motorbike, as she was narrowly missed by a bus!

SUDDEN DEATH

This case could have been prevented. I had been warning a client of mine repeatedly that they should avoid spending their time experimenting with new romantic relationships (I often do this, as spiritually there should ideally be a grace period before engaging with someone new), and instead focus their time on their work and their young children. My client was recently separated and the care of the young children was being shared between the father and the mother. On the day that the event took place, my client left the children at home with a teenage babysitter: the youngest child died instantly in a sudden and tragic accident, which could have been prevented had my client been at home. Parents should put their children first! This episode upset me a great deal as my client had been forewarned many times.

MENTAL HOSPITAL

This case should have been avoided. I had told the person in question, who was married to a nice man, not to get involved with a young man she was attracted to. It is human for people at times to be attracted to others, but if you are married, you should not act on the impulse unless you are ready to accept the karmic repercussions that will assail you as a result. It wasn't only because they were married, that I'd told them not to get involved with the young man: there were deeper, more serious reasons. I had been told and shown by The Divine why this would be a disastrous mistake for her to make. It had been revealed to me that the young man would end up leaving her penniless! And she was a wealthy lady when they first met. I went so far as to suggest to the lady to not sell her property if she were to go off with the young man, but she would not listen. I rarely keep on at someone if they are refusing to listen, but in this instance I did, as I was instructed to and the lady has goodness. The result of my warning her, ended up in my receiving a scathing letter from her and the young man, telling me to mind my own business. Some time passed and the young man left her for another woman who lived next door, leaving her penniless! The outcome was catastrophic, and with no money left, no property and nowhere to live, she suffered a mental collapse. Several of her friends, as well as her ex-husband, contacted me to tell me that she was now in a mental hospital. I pray that God will heal and assist her.

LEFT BEREFT

Words are powerful and ideally should be used wisely and with caution. A happy couple in their twenties had been introduced to me at a dinner party. The girl led the conversation initially, as her fiancé added polite small talk about travel and his work. The topic turned to their plans to marry in the coming weeks, and there was much excited chatter from the assembled guests, with everything from the wedding dress to the honeymoon discussed in joyful detail. Suddenly, the girl made a blasphemous statement, to the surprise of the dinner guests, which she followed by a stream of profanities! As I looked at her in shock, I felt an energy emerging from her that was most unpleasant. Everyone managed to laugh it off and switch the conversation back to lighter things, and the evening ended on a light note as we all left. Days later, on making the girl's acquaintance again, she had tear-stained cheeks as she blurted out that her fiancé had left her and called off their wedding, and that now she had nowhere to live as the property they were planning to start their married life in was his. I listened sympathetically, as she kept sobbing that she did not understand why this had happened. Then I heard The Divine speak to me, "It is karma brought on by her blaspheming!"

The following three case studies I am sharing for the sole purpose of expressing how The Divine, and our Angelic Helpers, are ever calling and stretching out with love, to assist, guide and encourage us, no matter what realm of existence we may be in, helping us to evolve into the Divine Beings we were created to be.

WARNING DREAMS

I agreed to take a call one day from a woman who wished to know if her daughter in spirit had gone over safely. The woman was very quietly spoken, and the energy was terribly low as she began speaking. I have spoken with many people who have similar questions but this felt different somehow. As I listened to her, it was suddenly revealed to me that her child had been abused and killed by her husband, whom she was still living with! When the abuse was taking place and her children were very young, the lady had been given clear and powerful dreams that her husband was abusing the children. Her husband could be a difficult man and at times was nasty, but she chose to dismiss the prophetic dreams and not act on them, thinking that perhaps she was being paranoid. A while later, after the dreams, one of her children mysteriously died. The woman suspected her husband but could not bring herself to confront him, as he could be violent. The years rolled on and only recently when her other children had grown up did they confess to her that her husband had abused them too. Hence her wish to speak with me now. The family was in tatters, with the woman utterly consumed with guilt and too afraid to confront her volatile husband. Her child's death could have been avoided and she knew it. Had she acted on the dreams being shown to her, and been brave enough to put her own neck on the line, instead of her children's, she could have put a stop to things before they got out of hand. It was now crystal clear that she had to confront and report her husband regardless of the consequences. Her daughter had gone over into spirit safely, but had left this world under terrible circumstances.

FORGIVENESS NEEDED

This case concerns a successful professional lady in the public eye who asked to be assisted to achieve stability in her public engagements and love life. As we began talking, an older relative of hers came through from spirit, keen to communicate with her. The energy I was getting from him was very strained. I was shown a scene from when the lady was a little girl, where she was with the older relative who is now in spirit. He was standing close to her and feeling remorseful. As I explained the scene to her, she told me how this relative, her grandfather, had sexually abused her when she was small. Her grandfather in spirit then expressed that he needed her forgiveness before he could move up spiritually. I explained this to the lady, who with compassion said that she harboured no resentment towards him, only confusion, since he had been loving and kind to her as she grew up. And she forgave him for sexually abusing her when she was young.

SAVED BY ANGELS

The person in question came to speak with me due to having been troubled by negative thought waves. As a young child, he had been gravely ill, and had spent much time in hospital. On one such occasion, as he lay in his hospital bed, the medics stood with looks of concern as they relayed to his parents that there was not much else that they could do for him. He recalled the medics and his parents then having left his little room to discuss matters. As he lay alone, frightened and in pain, a group of Angels appeared around his bed! The Angels smiled at him, and then began to operate on his body. He recalls them having made very high-pitched sounds as they communicated to one another during the procedure. The sounds they made were hurting his ears, and, noticing this, the Angels turned to apologise to him, explaining that they would lower their frequency so that the boy could understand and hear them without hurting his ears. They spoke gently then, in human language, and told him that he was going to be all right. They quickly finished the operation and left. He has not been unwell since. The experience has stayed with him his whole life and he is now a grown man, but since being in the loftiness of the presence of Angels, he has suffered with coping with the negative thought waves in this realm. I shared prayer techniques to assist him.

FINAL WORDS

My beloved boy lays by my side, along with my beloved girl, as I write these final words. My boy was returned to me again on earth, as promised, the night before the completion of my Sanctuary for God.

The three points regarding my life path still shrouded in mystery – my companion of God's choosing, my position in Eternity, and the promise I made to God – would all be made clear to me in the years to come, when I would eventually come to know that all relationships are an experiment leading us to the ultimate and eternal relationship, with God.

I live each day, immersed in the transcendent bliss of The Divine Love, which is unceasingly drawing us all forever upward into the heart of Unity. It is this true love that is born of compassion, that is ever transmuting the dark illusion of separateness. Its blazing light ever shining to empower the forces of good to triumph. Beckoning us to return to the higher, supremely good, spiritual life that was set for us from the beginning!

With pure motives for the manifestation of The Divine Plan – for all Beings to be in harmony with one another, and ultimately at one with God – I carry on between the worlds to fulfil God's Will, along with Em and Ray, as members of Yeshua's Team. Forever in the Eternal Now.

The third book of this *Modern Seer Trilogy* is to be put out into the public domain later on, in God's time.